LAST DAWN
THE HMS ROYAL OAK TRAGEDY AT SCAPA FLOW

THE WORLD WAR II BATTLESHIP

DAVID TURNER

ARGYLL ✠ PUBLISHING

© David Turner 2008
First published by Melrose Books, Ely, Cambridgeshire, an
imprint of Melrose Press, in 2004, under the title of
The Ultimate Sacrifice.

This edition published by
Argyll Publishing
Glendaruel
Argyll PA22 3AE
Scotland
www.argyllpublishing.com

The right of the author of this work has been asserted in
accordance with the Copyright, Designs and Patents Act of
1988.

British Library Cataloguing-in-Publication Data.
A catalogue record for this book is available from
the British Library.

ISBN 978 1906134 13 6

Printing: Bell & Bain Ltd, Glasgow

In memory of my late uncle
Commander Ralph Lennox Woodrow-Clark RN
1905-1939

This book is also dedicated to the many officers and men
who lost their lives; the survivors;
and their families and relatives.

They shall not grow old,
as we that are left grow old:
Age shall not weary them,
nor the years condemn.
At the going down of the sun,
and in the morning,
We will remember them.

Laurence Binyon

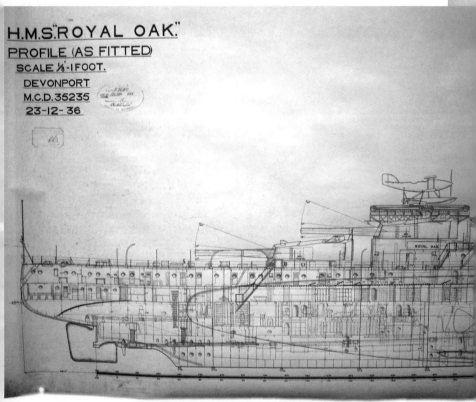

H.M.S."ROYAL OAK"
PROFILE (AS FITTED)
SCALE ⅛-1 FOOT.
DEVONPORT
M.C.D.35235
23-12-36

These pages and overleaf
Architectural drawing of HMS Royal Oak, stamped 1936, during
repair at her port of origin, Devonport.
The Royal Oak was laid down on 15th January, launched in 1914
and commissioned into the Royal Navy on 11th May 1916.
She saw service at the Battle of Jutland which proved to be the last
capital ship big fleet battle of the twentieth century.
Permission: National Maritime Museum

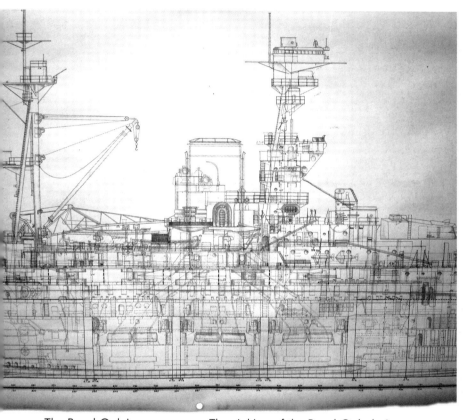

The Royal Oak is a war grave. The sinking of the Royal Oak during the early weeks of World War II was a national disaster. Although she was over twenty five years old, the battleship was considered to be robust and strong enough to resist enemy attack. This faith proved to be unfounded.

The Royal Oak was the last and largest battleship to be built at Devonport. She was nearly 600ft long with a maximum width of 100ft. She was armed with eight 15 inch guns contained in four

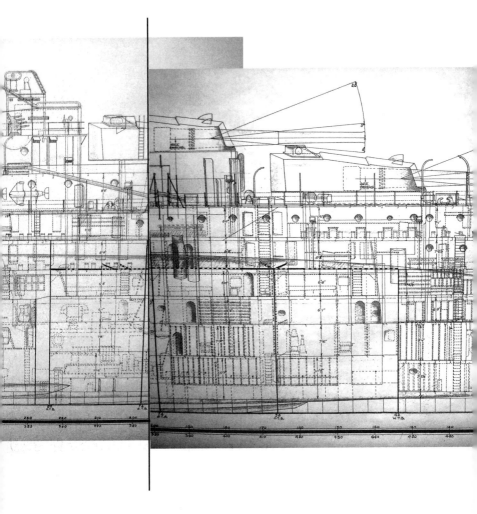

turrets, plus an assemblage of twelve 6-inch guns, eight 4-inch anti-aircraft guns and four 21-inch torpedo tubes. The warship was well armoured with 13 inches of steel that extended 5ft below her water line. She was capable of 20 knots at top speed powered by 40,000 horsepower oil-fuelled engines. A crew of nearly 1100 men was needed to handle her.

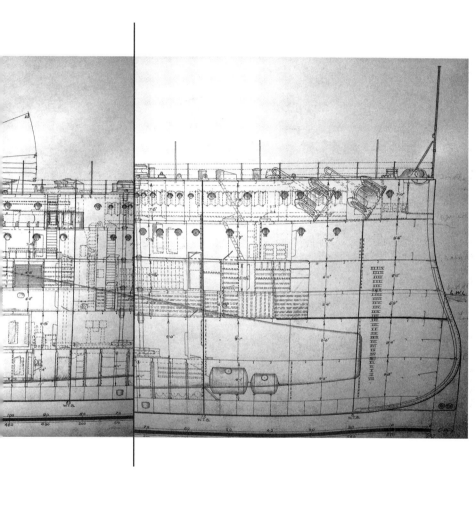

They that go down to the sea in ships,
and occupy their business in great waters,
These men see the works of the Lord
and his wonders in the deep.

CONTENTS

HMS Royal Oak

ILLUSTRATIONS

FOREWORD

Ships are the biggest mobile structures on Earth and to this status the battleship added another dimension. Battleships had to stay afloat in the face of attacks from torpedoes and bombing, mines and shells. In addition they had to withstand the tremendous shock of firing their own ordnance, as well as provide a home for their crew.

The battleship dominated the oceans for less than a century but left a legacy of action and power even after the disasters that showed how vulnerable they could be. A nation's strength was often determined by the number of its battleships. The aircraft carrier, a despised rival, usurped the position of a battleship as a capital ship within months of the outbreak of World War II. The battleships *Royal Oak, Prince of Wales* and *Repulse* had been sunk.

This book is the story of the first great tragedy of World War II, told to remember the 833 men of the battleship *Royal Oak* who made the supreme sacrifice on 14th October 1939. Her loss left parents, wives, children, families, mourning the loss of a dear son, loving husband, gentle father and close relative.

My uncle, Ralph Lennox Woodrow-Clark met his end that night on the *Royal Oak* and this book is dedicated to his memory.

David Turner
January 2008

Lieutenant Ralph Lennox Woodrow-Clark in dress uniform

Introduction

It was a dark and cold winter evening on 14th October 1939. I was nine years old and had arrived home from school to find my mother crying in the kitchen of our house at Laira in Plymouth.

I asked, "Why are you crying Mummy?" She told me that the BBC Home Service had reported late that morning an announcement by the Secretary to the Admiralty:

Ralph Lennox Woodrow-Clark – killed in action

> It is with regret that I have to announce that
> the battleship HMS *Royal Oak* has been sunk, it is believed
> by U-boat action, fifteen survivors have been landed.

My uncle, Ralph Lennox Woodrow-Clark, my mother's elder brother, was a senior officer on board the *Royal Oak* when she was torpedoed and sunk at Scapa Flow on 14th October 1939. His grave is in the Lyness Royal Navy Cemetery on the island of Hoy between Mill Bay and Ore Bay. Educated at the Royal Naval Colleges of Dartmouth and Greenwich, his future had promised promotion to the highest ranks within the Royal Navy.

I made a promise to my mother that one day I would visit his last resting place. It was to be a further 64 years before I was able to fulfill that promise.

The untimely death of my uncle became even more harrowing to his family and friends when it was known that he had been promoted to the rank of Commander and was due to take up a new post in one of His Majesty's Royal Navy capital ships.

LAST DAWN

H.M.S. *ROYAL OAK* INQUIRY[1]

Oral Answers House of Commons
17 October 1939 – 25 October 1939

Sir A Southby:
Asked the First Lord of the Admiralty when he expects to be in a position to make a further statement to the House regarding the loss of His Majesty's ship *Royal Oak*?

Mr Lambert:
Asked the first Lord of the Admiralty whether he can, consistent with the public interest, state the result of the inquiry instituted into the sinking of the *Royal Oak*.

THE FIRST LORD OF THE ADMIRALTY (Mr Churchill):
The inquiry into the causes of the loss of his Majesty's ship *Royal Oak* is now taking place as speedily as possible, but I cannot say when I shall be in a position to make a further statement as a result of the inquiry. I hope next week.

Mr Lambert:
Will my Right Hon. Friend make another statement as to the result?

Mr Churchill:
Yes, Sir; I will make another statement, but I shall have to be very careful not to disclose information which might be useful to other parties.

Sir A Southby:
While safeguarding the public interest, will my Right Hon. Friend bear in mind the very grave apprehension there is in the public mind regarding this matter?

Mr Churchill:
Yes, Sir, I will certainly bear that in mind.

Mr Ammon:
Is the committee of inquiry taking into consideration the fact that so large a number of men were drowned in harbour?

Sir Charles Cayzer:
Has the attention of my Right Hon. Friend been called to the statement made by the German U-Boat Commander himself that he waited for two days outside the harbour watching the track of vessels before he decided to go in?

Mr Churchill:
Yes, Sir, I have seen a number of statements made by the German U-Boat Commander. In fact they are a repetition of information which I have given to the House, and in fact they have no relation to the facts.

Mr Ammon:
Is attention being given to the fact that these men were drowned in harbour?

Mr Churchill:
Yes, Sir, but in relation to Scapa Flow, 'harbour' is not the right term, because it is a great land locked bay many miles across. This ship was several miles from any other vessel.

U-Boat Warfare

Mr A V Alexander:
(By private notice) asked the First Lord of the Admiralty whether he will make a statement in regard to the sinking of the battleship *Royal Oak*.

THE FIRST LORD OF THE ADMIRALTY (Mr Churchill):
The battleship *Royal Oak* was sunk at anchor by a U-Boat in Scapa Flow at approximately 1.30am on the 14th instant. It is still a matter of conjecture how the U-Boat penetrated the defences of the harbour. When we consider that during the whole course of the last war this anchorage was found to be immune from such attacks, on account of the obstacles imposed by the currents and the net barrages, this entry by a U-Boat must be considered as a remarkable exploit of professional skill and daring. A Board of Trade inquiry is now sitting at Scapa Flow to report on all that occurred, and anything that I say must be subject to revision in the light of their conclusions. It appears probable that the U-Boat fired a salvo of torpedoes at the *Royal Oak* of which only one hit the bow or anchor chain. This muffled explosion was at the time attributed to internal causes, and what is called the inflammable store, where the kerosene and other such materials are kept, was flooded. Twenty minutes later the U-Boat fired three more torpedoes and these striking in quick succession caused the ship to capsize and sink. She was lying at the extreme end of the harbour, and, therefore, many officers and men were drowned before rescue could be organised from other vessels. The lists of survivors have already been made public, and I deeply regret to inform the house that upwards of 800 officers and men have lost their lives. The Admiralty immediately announced the loss of this fine ship. Serious as this loss is, it does not affect the margin of security in heavy vessels which remains ample.

Meanwhile an intensive search of the anchorage has not yet yielded any results. It is clear, however, that after a certain time the harbour can be pronounced clear, as any U-Boat would have to rise to the surface for air or perish. All necessary measures are being taken to increase the precautions which in the late war proved effective. For the rest I must await the report of the Board which is now examining the event in full technical detail.

Mr Alexander:
May we on this side of the House join with the First Lord of the Admiralty in his general tribute to the personnel of the Royal Navy and the Mercantile Marine? May we also add our very deep sympathy with the relatives of those who have lost their lives in the sinking of the *Royal Oak*? May I ask the first Lord whether he is aware, as I am sure he must be, that the circumstances which he has been bound to report are very disturbing, and that perhaps we ought to know whether, at the outbreak of the war, there was or was not a systematic survey carried out at the place quoted to ensure that it still remained a safe naval anchorage? May I also ask whether we can be assured now that during the whole of the period since that survey there have been maintained properly at all times the boom defences required?

Mr Churchill:
Yes, Sir. The boom defences have been maintained and, of course, they are not the old defences from the last war, they have been newly placed in position. There is an inquiry sitting, which will not take very long, and I should like to have the advantage of reading its report before I go into details of this kind.

Commander Sir Archibald Southby:
Can the Right Hon. Gentleman say whether this German submarine was actually sighted inside Scapa Flow; and may I ask, further, whether as soon as the report is received he will give to the House as much information from the report as is consistent with the material safety?

Mr Churchill:

I did not say that the U-Boat was sighted inside Scapa Flow, but I have given the information which is in our possession according to the judgement we have been able to form in advance of the inquiry. When the inquiry is over I shall be ready, perhaps to answer some other questions if they will add to the information of the House.

Neville Chamberlain's War Cabinet in 1939
In the back row, reading from left to right, are: Sir Kingsley Wood (Secretary of State for Air); Winston Churchill (First Lord of the Admiralty); Leslie Hore-Belisha (Secretary of State for War); and Lord Hankey (Minister without Portfolio).
Seated in front, from left to right, are Lord Halifax (Foreign Secretary); Sir John Simon (Chancellor of the Exchequer); Neville Chamberlain (Prime Minister); Sir Samuel Hoare (Lord Privy Seal); and Lord Chatfield (Minister for the Co-ordination of Defence).

HIS MAJESTY'S GOVERNMENT
(Formed by the Right Hon. Neville Chamberlain, September 1939)[2]

WAR CABINET
Prime Minister and First Lord of the Treasury –
Rt. Hon. Neville Chamberlain
Chancellor of the Exchequer –
Rt. Hon. Sir John Simon, G.C.S.I., G.C.V.O., OBE,
KG. MP
Secretary of State for Foreign Affairs –
Rt. Hon. Viscount Halifax. K.G., G.C.S.I., G.C.I.E.
Minister for Co-ordination of Defence T.D. Admiral of the Fleet –
Rt. Hon. Lord Chatfield G.C.B., O.M., K.G.M.G.,
C.V.O.
First Lord of the Admiralty –
Rt. Hon. Winston Leonard Spencer Churchill,
CH.MP
Secretary of State for War –
Rt. Hon. Leslie Hore-Belisha, MP
Secretary of State for Air –
Rt. Hon. Sir H Kingsley Wood MP
Lord Privy Seal –
Rt. Hon. Sir Samuel Hoare, Bt., G.C.S.I., G.B.E.,
C.H.G., MP
Minister without Portfolio –
Rt. Hon. Lord Hankey, G.C.B., G.C.M.G.,
G.C.V.O.

Notes
1. From House of Lords Record Office, The Parliamentary Archives,
London SWIA OPW
2. From House of Lords Record Office

HMS Royal Oak
Permission: The Trustees of the Imperial War Museum, London Q 018144

Letter of Condolence sent to the widow
of Ralph Lennox Woodrow-Clark from Captain Benn

Chapter 1

THE LOST YEARS

My first visit to Scapa Flow was in September 2003 to visit my uncle's war grave. The contents of the subsequent programme broadcast for BBC Radio Orkney are mentioned in Chapter 7.

The BBC during that programme were kind enough to carry out a search in an attempt to locate my cousin Michael, the son of Commander Ralph Lennox Woodrow-Clark RN but without success. The electoral roll did not mention his name.

Recently, however, I received the sad news that Michael Woodrow-Clark passed away in July 1994 aged just 63 years. He was a Marine Engineer (retired) with the Esso Oil Company. On 12th April 2006 I made the journey to Didcot Oxon to meet my cousin's wife and daughter who I have not had contact with for thirty years. I was told that my uncle's wife Marjorie had died in Plymouth in 1997 aged 72 years.

It came as quite a surprise to learn that my uncle's wife's dying wish was to have her ashes scattered on her husband's grave within the Navy Cemetery at Lyness, Orkney. Her ashes are currently in the safekeeping of my cousin's daughter. Her wishes will be honoured in due course. I extend my thanks to them within the confines of this book for allowing me to publish additional information concerning my uncle's career leading up to his appointment to the battleship *Royal Oak* at Devonport on 24th April 1939.

Left is a letter of condolence written to my uncle's wife on 29th

"Belstone"
Dousland
S. Devon.
Oct 19th 1939.

Dear Mr Clarke.

It is with the deepest regret we learned the sad news of the loss of your husband, and my wife & I offer our sincere & heartfelt sympathy.

As you know, your husband & I were very intimate & he was a fine shipmate and a great friend. It is hard to realise that he, & so many other colleagues have passed on. But for my wife's illness, I should have been in the ship with them all. They have made the supreme sacrifice, but although time will dull the wound, their friendship & love will always be a bright memory.

It is a great blow for you & I pray you will have strength to bear the affliction. Please remember me to his father, I think he will remember "Bish" as The Senior" always called me.

Believe me,

Your very sincerely
AWMandall

Chaplain R.N.

Letter from U W Mandall, Chaplain RN

October 1939, fifteen days after the sinking of the *Royal Oak,* signed W.G Benn. W.G Benn was captain of the warship on the night she sank and was some time later promoted to the rank of Rear Admiral. No doubt he was taking a holiday following the tragedy.

It is interesting to note that the Captain and my uncle were together at the time of the first explosion examining the best means of coping with the situation.

Yet another letter of condolence was received by my uncle's wife, from friends, dated 19th October 1939, five days after the sinking of the *Royal Oak*. I have selected this particular letter for inclusion, because but for his wife's illness her husband would also have been on the battleship at the time of her sinking, serving as a Chaplain RN.

Letter from Admiralty

.W.20121/39

17th October, 1939.

Madam,

In confirmation of Admiralty telegram of the 14th October, I am commanded by My Lords Commissioners of the Admiralty to state that they have been informed that your husband, Lieutenant (E) Ralph Lennox Woodrow Clark, Royal Navy is presumed to have lost his life in the sinking of H.M.S. ROYAL OAK on 14th October.

My Lords desire to express to you their deep regret at receiving this intelligence and their profound sympathy in your great loss.

I am, Madam,

Your obedient Servant,

R.H.Marti

Mrs. M.E. Clark,
    4, Mutley Park Villas,
        Plymouth.
            Devon.

A letter dated 17th October 1939 from the Lords Commissioners
of the Admiralty states that my uncle is presumed to have lost his
life in the sinking of HMS *Royal Oak* on 14th October. As we now
know his body was recovered on 15th October.

This letter from the Lords Commissioners of the Admiralty states
that my uncle was buried with full naval honours in the Lyness
Naval War Cemetery, on the island of Hoy, in the Orkney Islands. I
must assume that the other twenty-five buried there also received
this honour irrespective of their rank.

The letter opposite written from Buckingham Palace to my
uncle's wife and signed by King George VI, not dated but presumed
1939, needs no further explanation.

L.P.—No. 8.

Any further communication
should be addressed to—

The Secretary of the Admiralty,
London, S.W.1.

quoting "_N.L._ "

Admiralty, S.W.1.

23rd November, *19* 39.

Madam,

      I am commanded by My Lords Commissioners
of the Admiralty to inform you that a report has
now been received that your husband, the late
Lieut.(E) R.L.W.Clark,R.N., was buried with Naval
Honours in Lyness War Cemetery, Orkneys.

      I am, Madam,

      Your obedient Servant,

rs.M.E.Clark,
  4, Mutley Park Villas,
    Plymouth,
      DEVON.

BUCKINGHAM PALACE

The Queen and I offer you our heartfelt sympathy in your great sorrow.

We pray that your country's gratitude for a life so nobly given in its service may bring you some measure of consolation.

George R.I

Mrs. H.E. Clarke,
   4, Mutley Park Villas,
     Plymouth,
      Devon.

Letter from George VI

Jan 16th 1921
On board H.M.S.
Indus
Devonport.

Jan 16th 1922
On board H.M.S.
Indus.
Devonport

Jan 16th 1923
On board H.M.S.
Frigard, Portsmouth

Jan 16th. 1924
On board H.M.S
Frigard
Portsmouth

Jan 16th 1925
On board H.M.S.
Frigard
Portsmouth

Jan 16th 1926
H.M.S Ramillies
Atlantic Fleet.

Friday Jan 16th 1920.
First met Marjorie, took
me home after the concert.

Jan 16th 1927
H.M.S Steadfa . .
Bound for China

Chapter 2

THE LIFE OF RALPH LENNOX WOODROW-CLARK, RN

The information opposite, dated 16th January 1927 is written on the back of a concert programme. This was the occasion that Ralph Woodrow-Clark first met his wife-to-be Marjorie. He made a list on the programme by request, of some of the ships in which he served, from when he first joined the fleet from Naval College.

One can deduce from the various dates that they did not in those days serve on one ship for long periods. On the right is the list of some of the ships to which my uncle was repaired.

Commander Ralph Lennox Woodrow-Clark RN was an accomplished artist and probably a frustrated journalist, although he had many articles published in various magazines of the day writing under the name of Ralph Woodrow. Included overleaf is something which appeared in *The Fleet* in June 1934, together with his drawing in pen and ink of the battleship *Iron Duke*, a ship in which he served.

In spite of long enforced absences away from his wife and son, due to his chosen career as a Naval Officer, the following letters written on board ship to his son Michael (sometimes referred to as John) denote what a devoted father he truly was.

These letters are but a few chosen from many – unfortunately all are undated. They include the very first letter written to my uncle from his son. In spite of war and conflict, we are all human

ANOTHER "VICTORY"?

BY RALPH WOODROW

THE preservation of H.M.S. "Victory"—throughout a century and more—provided us with a tangible link 'twixt our own age and that of the great seaman Admiral Lord Nelson. Have we any famous warship—rich in historic associations—which might fittingly be handed on to posterity as the symbol of this age which knew the Great War? Many senior Naval officers have been heard to suggest—in their more private discussions—that H.M.S. "Iron Duke" should be preserved for this purpose. What claims may be voiced in support of this particular ship and its active associations with famous men and great occasions?

The name "Iron Duke" has been borne by only one other warship of the Royal Navy, that being an armour-plated battleship launched at Pembroke in 1870. This former "Iron Duke" achieved some notoriety in that she rammed and sank H.M.S. "Vanguard" off the Kish Bank in the Irish Channel in 1875. She also flew the flag of Vice-Admiral Shadwell when that officer was Commander-in-Chief of the China Station. Rendered non-effective in 1901 she was sold out of the Service five years later.

The present "Iron Duke" was launched on the 12th October, 1912, by the late Duchess of Wellington, wife of the fourth Duke. The ship commissioned for trials in March 1914, and the Great War had commenced when she became a real fighting unit. First of the long list of famous men who were to hoist their flag in H.M.S. "Iron Duke" was Admiral Callaghan. He was followed by Admiral Jellicoe, and thus the vessel under discussion became flagship of the Grand Fleet and her name received world-wide recognition as the foremost ship of the greatest assemblage of Naval power that history can record. At Jutland the "Iron Duke" performed well as Fleet flagship and as a fighting unit. When subsequent to Jutland another encounter with the German Fleet seemed imminent, Admiral Jellicoe, in a dispatch of August 1916, expressed himself as follows: "On the assumption that the enemy would turn to the eastward on meeting us, I directed a concentration fire of ships that would be ahead of 'Iron Duke' on deployment of two ships to one, leaving 'Iron Duke' to deal with

one ship singly as a compliment to her accurate firing Jutland."

Admiral Beatty was the next famous personage to hoist flag aboard "Iron Duke."

The re-organisation of our Fleets after the Great War fou H.M.S. "Iron Duke" flagship of the Mediterranean Fle where she remained until 1926. During this period of serv in the "Middle Sea" she carried the flags of Admirals Somerset Gough Calthorpe, Sir John Robeck and Sir Osmo de B. Brock; Vice-Admiral Sir Michael Hodges and Re Admiral Hugh Watkins. On rejoining the then Atlantic Fl she was in turn the flagship of Rear-Admirals F. H. Mitch R. Backhouse, R. Thompson and J. Casement.

The stringent provisions of the much-criticised Lond Treaty was a cruel blow to the former flagship of the Gra Fleet. She was stripped of her armour, deprived of two g turrets, and had her machinery so adjusted as to reduce maximum speed to some 18 knots. In this state of demilita ation she still renders invaluable service as the gunnery train ship of the Royal Navy. It may well prove that in this capa she will add further to her fame as the cradle of future gunn experts. Yet it must be remembered that H.M.S. "Iron Du is now in the twenty-second year of a very strenuous existe and her future as an active unit cannot be as lengthy as mi be desired. What is to happen to this famous flagship? Is to know the day when—in the hands of the shipbreakers will be written of her, as of so many others—

> "O mighty Caesar, dost thou lie so low?
> Are all thy conquests, glories, triumphs, spoils,
> Shrunk to this little measure"?

Or, happier thought, will this generation follow the example that which realised the meaning and lesson of Trafalgar thus preserve the "Iron Duke" to be another "Victory"? would indeed appear desirable that this course be adop and the flagship of Lord Jellicoe and many another fam admiral be preserved to posterity, the witness of the Nav part in the Great War, when Britain's proud claim to be kno as "Mistress of the Seas" was upheld before the world.

and act as such. Through these written words of a very private family man, one of so many whose lives were cut short on the *Royal Oak*, his being and his actions will live on.

> H.M.S. *Royal Oak*
> Portland.
> Sunday
>
> Dear Michael,
>
> I do hope your cold is better. Mummy tells me that she has one as well. We are at Portland now with the rest of the Home Fleet. When I come home again with the ship you shall come onboard. She is bigger than the *Iron Duke*. You will be going to school next week. I think you will like it. Work hard and take care of mummy for me wont you.
>
> Cheerio old man heaps of love and kisses
> from Daddy.

> DEAR DADDY COME HOME SOON. I LOVE YOU.
> JOHN
> x x x
>
> John's first letter writen 10.2.15.

Dear John, I hope you will like
this ship. I am so sorry that
the last one was going the wrong
way. I hope you'll like the
Bull Dog I am enclosing, he has
just joined Dartmouth.

Mummy tells me you have been
very poorly in your tummy. I am
ever so sorry & do hope that you
are better.

I hope you are still being
good boy & taking great care
dear mummy for me. I shall
will be able to take me out
again & see the trains & go for
bus rides. I don't see any
trains out here.

Goodnight my son . heaps
of love & kisses from

XXX
XXX
XXX

Dear John,

Thank you ever ever so much for your lovely letter. It was ever so nice & I think you are such a clever boy.

I shall soon be coming home to see you again & dear mammy. Take care of her for me please won't you, because she is ever so precious, & so is my dear boy John.

Tell grandad & grandma that I think you are a very clever boy & you shall have a lovely time when I come home again.

Goodnight now, & off to bed. Lots & lots of big loves & kisses from daddy

Please give mammy a kiss for me.

x x x x x x x
x x x x xxx

XXX

The letter instructing my uncle to repair on board the *Royal Oak* at Devonport on 24th April 1939 is interesting in as much that it informs that his tenure on board the battleship was to be brief. A much more significant fact is that it was an amended appointment, the intention having been to repair to a different ship, name unknown and not included within his service records.

C.W.

Amended appointment

By Command of the Commissioners for Executing the Office of Lord High Admiral of the United Kingdom, &c.

To Lieutenant (E) R. L. W. Clarke R.N

THE Lords Commissioners of the Admiralty hereby appoint you Lieutenant (E), of His Majesty's Ship *Royal Oak*

and direct you to repair on board that Ship at Devonport on 24th April 1939. Your appointment is to take effect from that date.

You are to acknowledge the receipt of this Appointment *forthwith*, addressing your letter to the Commanding Officer, H.M.S. *Royal Oak* taking care to furnish your address.

25 Cranbourne Avenue Plymouth

By Command of their Lordships,

Admiralty, S.W.1. 18th April 1939.

(8/8/38) (434) Wt. 43311/4873 5m 3/39 S.E.R. Ltd. Gp. 671

Launching of the Royal Oak – HM Dockyard Devonport – by Viscountess Vallatort with Mr Hockaday (Manager of Construction, Devonport Dockyard) and Admiral Manday

Chaplain's service prior to launching Royal Oak in 1914 Both photographs reproduced here by courtesy of the Plymouth Naval Base Museum

HMS Royal Oak in line astern

Chapter 3

THE SINKING OF THE *ROYAL OAK*

In June 1939, after a visit to Torbay, the *Royal Oak* sailed into Devonport, the port of her construction, where the crew were issued with tropical clothing in the belief they were going to the Mediterranean. However, as World War II seemed inevitable, the *Royal Oak* was ordered to sail to Scapa Flow in the Orkney Islands. At 11:15am on 3rd September 1939, Prime Minister Chamberlain made a sad and uninspired broadcast to tell the nation they were at war.

On the evening of 15th September 1939, Winston Churchill boarded a London train with Lieutenant Commander C.R ('Tommy') Thompson, the first Lord's Flag Commander. Their destination was off the north coast of Scotland: the anchorage of Britain's home fleet in the sea basin of Scapa Flow. There, if anywhere, Churchill thought, the Royal Navy should be buttoned up. Later, he recalled how 'on two or three occasions' in the autumn of 1914, most memorably on 17th October, 'The alarm was given that there was a U-boat inside the anchorage. Guns were fired, destroyers thrashed the waters, and the whole gigantic armada put out to sea in haste and dudgeon.' Scapa was that important.

Anxiety over the sea basin had returned and this time the threat was real. In Churchill's lap lay a locked box of secret documents, among them a shocking report from the Chiefs of Staff Committee revealing that Scapa's defences would not be ready until the Spring of 1940. Upon arrival he called on Sir Charles Forbes, the

HMS Royal Oak

HMS Royal Oak fires her massive guns

HMS Royal Oak crew portrait

Commander in Chief, aboard HMS *Nelson*, the Admiral's flagship. Sir Charles confirmed that the basin's entrance channels were 'not properly netted'. The old steel webs had rusted, rotted, broken up, and drifted away. Churchill immediately issued an order, stamped 'urgent', calling for nets, booms, blockships (sunken ships barring entrance channels), anti-aircraft guns, patrol craft, balloons and searchlights. Until they were in place, Scapa was insecure, an inviting target for daring German submarine commanders.

After the outbreak of war in 1939, German reconnaissance aircraft took photographs over Scapa Flow of British ships at anchor and the state of the harbour defences. These were passed to Kommodore Karl Dönitz, commodore of the *Unterseeboote* arm of the *Kriegsmarine*, ultimately to become an Admiral, Deputy *Führer*, and for a brief time, *Führer*.

After studying the photographs and reports, Dönitz decided that, given the right man, a U-boat could attack the British fleet base and sink some of her still mighty capital ships.

U-boat Kapitäns, so successful in sinking merchant ships were now turning their periscopes towards Britain's ships of war. It was disquieting to know that Kommodore Karl Dönitz's vessels were lurking in British waters, capable of striking one of His Majesty's capital ships at any hour. Churchill's anxiety over Scapa Flow continued.

It is well known that two U-boats had attempted to penetrate the deep, almost landlocked basin during World War I and neither had returned but, studying aerial photographs of the anchorage in 1939, Dönitz reached the conclusion that an adroit navigator could thread his way past the three sunken ships meant to block Holm Sound. The opportunity was given to Kapitän-leutnant Günther Prien to command the VHB type U-boat, *U-47*.

Prien was his best U-boat Kapitän and he almost failed. It took him nearly six hours to do it – at one point he seemed hopelessly ensnared in a cable from one of the block-ships.

The German U-boat *U-47* sailed under Prien's command from her base at Kiel on Sunday 8th October 1939 – destination Scapa Flow! On that day, the *Royal Oak*, accompanied by two screening

HMS Royal Oak crew photographed under her guns

HMS Royal Oak in Pentland Firth

HMS Royal Oak in Portsmouth Harbour before the start of World War II

HMS Royal Oak

destroyers, was patrolling the channel between Fair Isle and Orkney. Her mission was to prevent the German battlecruiser *Gneisenau* from breaking into the Atlantic and attacking the merchant convoys that supplied Britain.

The *Gneisenau* had been reported off Norway and the British battle-cruisers *Hood* and *Repulse*, together with the newest battle-ships, *Nelson* and *Rodney* and the aircraft carrier *Furious*, with scouting and screening destroyers, had set off across the North Sea to intercept her, leaving *Royal Oak* to close the gap between Orkney and Shetland. There were tremendous gales during the next day or so and even a ship the size of *Royal Oak* suffered in the violent seas. Massive waves swept along her forecastle deck, damaging fittings and carrying away Carley life rafts, with water severely flooding the battery deck. The *Royal Oak* was ordered back to port and arrived back in Scapa Flow on 11th October. Rather than leave the capital ships in Scapa Flow they had been sent away to protect them from Luftwaffe attacks.

The *Royal Oak* was ordered to the north-east of the anchorage where her anti-aircraft guns could protect the important radio direction-finding station at Netherbutton near Kirkwall. As *U-47* continued its mission to penetrate Scapa Flow, the crew of the *Royal Oak* spent Friday 13th October clearing up the shambles below decks after her rough passage earlier in the week. She also took stores on board.

All that day, *U-47* was lying on the bottom of the North Sea, 90 metres down, some miles to the east of the Orkney Islands.

On the night of 13th and 14th October 1939, *U-47* penetrated the line of block ships in Kirk Sound and found the old battleship *Royal Oak* lying at anchor before her, bows to the north-east along both the direction of wind and the eddy current set up in Scapa Bay by the ebbing tide.

Prien's first salvo of three torpedoes fired from ahead failed to do any damage, for the one torpedo that did hit apparently struck an anchor chain or detonated only partially. After an interval to reload, Prien fired another salvo and this time there was a loud explosion underneath the *Royal Oak* and she rolled over and sank

Winston Churchill

within minutes. By 01:30, all that was to be seen of the *Royal Oak* was fuel oil and men desperately fighting for their lives. A total of 833 men died with her.

It has been said that she was destroyed by a colossal explosion, but Admiralty records show only that the ship capsized and sank after heavy flooding amidships. The loss of 24 officers and 809 men was much greater than it need have been because the ship's company had not yet become accustomed to war routine.

No doubt feeling secure in a quiet corner of the anchorage, the ship's officers had not ensured that all the watertight doors and hatches were closed and so the ship was at her most vulnerable. The *Royal Oak* was only fit for second-line duties, but the skill of Prien and his *U-47* in penetrating a base that had been thought to be impregnable shook the confidence of the Admiralty. As in 1914, the Home Fleet had been sent away to bases on the west coast of Scotland until the defences could be strengthened.

The Royal Navy reacted quickly. On 15th October, nets were spread over the wreck to catch any floating bodies. Divers went down to inspect the wreck. Some ascended in horror at the sight of the suspended bodies that they encountered. Men were found jammed in the portholes as they tried in desperation to get out of the wreck. The decision was taken immediately to place three further block ships in Kirk Sound.

It was not then known how *U-47* had got in and this action demonstrated that the precise weaknesses in the defences had been recognised even before the *Royal Oak* tragedy. The attack infuriated Churchill. He ordered the construction of barriers. The Churchill

Kapitänleutnant
Günther Prien

barriers, as they were named, were sufficiently high in 1942 to prevent any repetition of the *Royal Oak* incident. They were completed in 1944.

The following detailed account does not appear in the Admiralty records and is as recounted to the author by an unknown survivor of the tragedy, who wishes to remain anonymous.

> A torpedo from the *U-47* scored a direct hit on the *Royal Oak's* starboard side, another torpedo started a fire in the magazine, while yet another blew a huge hole in the engine room. Almost immediately, the mighty battleship that had fought at the Battle of Jutland in 1916 keeled over 45 degrees and went to the sea-bed. The inferno on board destroyed the crowded mess decks, taking a heavy toll of boy seamen, ratings and Royal Marines: some, burned and suffering from shock, ran through flames to jump into the sea. Down below, in the confined machinery spaces and boiler room, stokers fought blindly to escape the choking smoke and scalding steam, but many of the steel ladders buckled in the intense heat preventing the men from escaping.

At 02:15, *U-47* slipped out of Scapa Flow and headed for home, reaching Wilhelmshaven on 17th October 1939 at 11:44. The crew were given a heroes' welcome and they were flown to Berlin where Günther Prien was awarded the Knight's Cross, Germany's highest honour, and the whole crew took lunch with Hitler.

It is now a known fact, that the Royal Navy was officially aware of the gaps in the defences at Kirk Sound. When *Royal Oak* arrived at Scapa just before the outbreak of war, one of her officers, a submariner temporarily seconded to the battleship, had surveyed the harbour's defences and had reported in writing that he was certain that he could navigate a small submarine through Kirk Sound. *Royal Oak's* navigator made an independent examination of the channel and came to the same conclusion.

Even before then the Navy had designated an old steamer to act as a fourth blockship to completely seal off Kirk Sound, but in a supreme irony, the intended blockship was sunk by a U-boat on its way north.

Within days, an account of the sinking of *Royal Oak*, attributed to Prien, was in print and selling out in German bookstores. This hastily crafted account was based on *U-47's* log and Prien's recollections, so it included all the errors he had made that night such as believing he had seen and torpedoed *Repulse* and that there had been destroyers present inshore of *Royal Oak*.

Many have used the inconsistencies in Prien's log to make the case that Prien was never in Scapa Flow and that *Royal Oak* sank due to sabotage. The Royal Navy announced that the cause of *Royal Oak's* sinking was a U-boat before they had explicit evidence that this was the case. In spite of possible evidence to the contrary the Royal Navy maintained the story for propaganda reasons. According to the theory, admitting a sinking by U-boat was far less damaging to public morale than the acknowledgement of sabotage, which would have been disastrous.

The Germans, according to this line of reasoning, were only too willing to go along with the Admiralty line, because it protected their saboteurs and did wonders for the image of their U-boat arm.

Churchill was informed immediately of the sinking of the *Royal Oak* and the loss of 833 officers and men, among them Captain W.G. Benn and Rear Admiral H.E.C. Blagrove (Commander of the 2nd Battle Squadron).

When told, Churchill said, 'Poor fellows, poor fellows, trapped in those black depths.'

He wept, then thought of the unknown submariners' achievement and murmured 'what a wonderful feat of arms'.

The sinking of the *Royal Oak* was one of the biggest disasters of World War II.

Due to bad communication, Churchill had been told, in error, that the captain was lost with the ship. At a subsequent Admiralty Board of Enquiry, Captain Benn was called to give evidence about the tragedy.

When the image of a U-Boat commander is called to mind, it will always be that of Günther Prien. A man of great courage and initiative, but of very narrow focus, he was ideally suited to the task of taking a slender steel cylinder to sea and directing it against the enemy

Chapter 4

KAPITÄNLEUTNANT GÜNTHER PRIEN
AND THE U-BOOTWAFFE

'The only thing that ever really
frightened me during the war
was the U-boat peril'
Winston Churchill

Germany's World War II U-boat fleet was a truly elite fighting force. The *U-bootwaffe* represented the cream of German naval personnel and in training, technology, tactics and combat successes, the German fleet was far superior to that of any other combatant nation. In spite of this, losses of crew members in World War II were between 75 and 80 per cent. Few members of any elite formation sacrificed so many of their number in battle as the members of the German *U-bootwaffe*.

Günther Prien – Born 16th January 1908 Osterfeld, Thüringen
Died 7th March 1941 North Atlantic
30 ships sunk for a total of 162,769 GRT
1 warship sunk for a total of 29,150 tons
8 ships damaged for a total of 62,751 GRT

55

Günther Prien became a sailor at the age of fifteen and by 1923 he was an officer in the Hamburg Amerika Line. In 1933 Prien joined the German Navy. In 1938 he was given command of *U-47*. Two years after sinking HMS *Royal Oak* Prien was credited with destroying 28 merchant ships.

After the war, a significant number of successful U-boat commanders went on to join the post-war West German Navy and served again with great distinction, reaching high rank in NATO working alongside their former foes.

1941 saw Joachim Schepke killed in action and Otto Kretschmer captured by the British and imprisoned in Britain and Canada for seven years. He was later to become Chief of Staff of the NATO Command Comenavbaltap at Kiel in May 1965. He retired in September 1970 as a Flotillen Admiral.

In that one year Germany had lost three of its top aces. Günther Prien remained the greatest hero because his sinking of the battleship *Royal Oak* at Scapa Flow in *U-47* was the *U-Bootwaffe's* first major success. Kapitänleutnant Günther Prien, probably the most famous of the *U-bootwaffe's* ace commanders, was killed in action in 1941.

U-47 leaves Kiel for Scapa Flow, 8th October 1939

U-47 had a displacement of 761 metric tonnes; 865 tonnes submerged.

She was powered by two 1400 PS (IMW) Diesel engines and two 375 PS (KW) electric motors. Her speed was 17 knots (31km/hr) on the surface and 7.6 knots (14km/hr) submerged.

Her underwater armament comprised four torpedo tubes in the bow and one torpedo tube in the stern. The deck artillary was an 88mm gun and a 20mm machine gun. Range was 6500 nautical miles (12,000km)

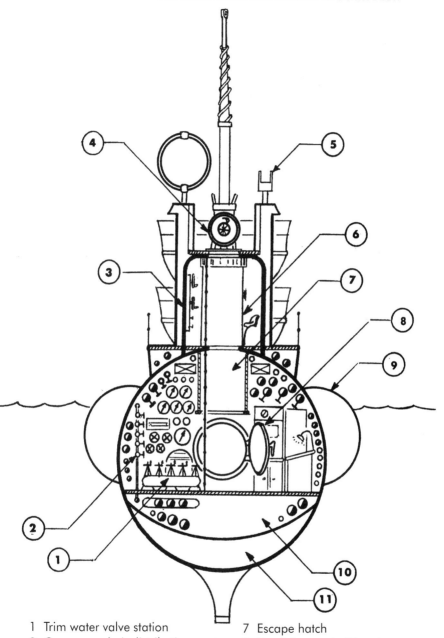

1 Trim water valve station
2 Compressed air distribution centre
3 Tower compartment with computer
4 Bridge hatch with lid
5 Radar warning device
6 Periscope housing

7 Escape hatch
8 Hatch in rear bulkhead
9 Saddle tanks
10 Control room bilge
11 Boyancy tank No 3

U-Boat Losses, 1939-1945

	1939	1940	1941	1942	1943	1944	1945
January		1	-	3	6	15	13
February		5	-	2	19	20	22
March		-	5	6	15	25	34
April		7	2	3	15	21	57
May		1	1	4	41	23	28
June		-	4	3	17	25	
July		2	1	12	37	23	
August		3	3	9	25	34	
September	2	-	2	10	9	23	
October	4	1	2	16	26	12	
November	2	3	5	13	19	8	
December	1	-	10	15	8	12	
Totals	9	22	35	96	237	241	153
Grand total							793*

* includes U-505 and U-570 which were captured on the high seas
Of 842 U-boats launched, 779 were sunk, 'iron coffins' to 28,000 men.

The U-bootwaffe represented the cream of German Naval personnel.
Few members of any elite formation sacrificed so many of their
number in battle as the members of the German U-bootwaffe

Map of Scapa Flow

U-47 heading for its target

There is no doubt that Günther Prien of *U-47 was* the best known U-Boat commander of World War II, largely because he achieved the impossible and spectacular by taking his boat through the defences of the renowned British Naval Base at Scapa Flow and sinking the battleship *Royal Oak*.

It was Engelbert Endress, Prien's first watch officer in *U-47*, who was responsible for 'loosing' the salvo of torpedoes which sank the *Royal Oak*. He was eventually promoted to command *U-46*, sinking 26 Allied ships totalling 142,000 tons.

Only one other U-Boat commander had a record that surpassed Prien. He was Otto Kretschmer in *U-99* – his tally was 44 ships totalling 226,000 tons plus a destroyer.

It has been alleged by some that following discrepancies within Prien's log on the night of 14th October 1939 that Prien and *U-47* were not in Scapa Flow on this date and that the battleship was sunk by another U-Boat.

I now have a letter in my possession from a former watch officer of a U-Boat stating that Prien and his boat *U-47* did sink the battleship *Royal Oak*, which really places the matter beyond doubt. Infomation within the U-Boat Archiv, Cuxhaven-Altenbrach Museum states: 'The allegation that Prien and his boat *U-47* sank the battleship *Royal Oak* is true.'

It would seem that today in Germany the generation involved in World War II in some instances are still marked as criminals. Many of the descendants of highly decorated men are ashamed about their forebears and do not want to discuss the events of World War II and their parents' or grandparents' participation. Prien completed an almost impossible task successfully. Could he have achieved this without help?

A good many of the original crew of *U-47* died when she sank in the North Atlantic in 1941 with the loss of all hands. Others who had been in *U-47* with Prien at Scapa Flow had been appointed to other U-Boats between October 1939 and 1941 and did not suffer the fate of *U-47*. However, a good many of the crew of *U-47* did die during the war albeit in other U-Boats. The photograph on page 65 from an unknown source, proves that some of the crew of *U-47*

U-47 entering Krupp's dockyards

Prien's Mad Bull insignia on the conning tower. His insignia was adopted by the 7th U-flotilla (Courtesy of Mark Bentley, Tiger Collectibles, 2004)

The crew of U-47 were given a welcome fit for heroes when they arrived at the airport in Berlin after sinking the Royal Oak

Crowds gathered in the streets of Berlin to
welcome the crew of the U-47 after she
returned from sinking the Royal Oak

Thousands of people lined the route of the
victory parade held in honour of the crew
of the U-47 when she returned to
Germany after sinking the Royal Oak

Hitler congratulates
Kapitänleutnant
Günther Prien

Prien and the crew of the U-47
dine with Hitler

returned to Scapa flow many years later, certainly after 1942. It strains credulity, therefore, to believe that Prien was never in Scapa Flow or that they could have maintained a fiction concerning that mission, as some in the past have claimed it to have been for all these years since the end of the war.

Prien found himself in the spotlight again after having sunk the *Royal Oak*, this time for a different reason some weeks later when *U-47* attacked three large transports and the battleship *Warspite* without success, the fault not being with Prien and *U-47*, but with unpredictable and unreliable German torpedoes. On many occasions U-Boats made attacks on important British warships, including major battleships, only for the torpedoes to either run wild or fail to explode on impact.

In June 1940 Prien attacked several convoys and sank six ships before running out of torpedoes, and in October 1940 he led four U-Boats in an attack on another convoy and sank fourteen ships, ultimately becoming the first U-Boat commander to sink 200,000 tons of enemy shipping and consequently receiving the highest possible decoration of the Oak Leaves to add to his Knight's Cross.

On 7th March 1941 Prien was shadowing convoy OB-293 but was spotted by the British destroyer *Wolverine* commanded by Lt Cdr J M Rowland. *U-47* crash dived as *Wolverine's* depth charges thrashed the sea. The U-Boat's propeller was badly damaged and the noise it created was a constant indication to the *Wolverine* of its position. Another depth-charge attack was sufficient to put a final end to Prien and *U-47* with all hands. Prien had sunk 28 merchant ships. However, the loss of Prien, and also of U-Boat Kapitäns Schepke and Kretshmer within a few weeks of each other, marked the beginning of the end of the good times for U-Boatmen.

greeted by Admiral Saalwachter upon his return from sinking HMS Royal Oak in Scapa Flow. More elaborate greetings followed, including a trip to Berlin and dinner with Hitler.

ceremony, taken a few previous, when U-47 alongside the quay in Wilhelmshaven, 17th Oct

Article in British newspaper on Prien

U-47 docking after a patrol in November 1940 at Lorient. This was at the height of the good times for U-Boat warfare, when a few boats under skilled, experienced Commanders were achieving enormous successes against weakly guarded convoys. Note the 'Bull of Scapa Flow' insignia, thought up by Prien's then number two, Engelbert Endrass, as U-47 was returning to Germany after sinking the Battleship Royal Oak. It was adopted as the insignia of the 7th Flotilla, to which U-47 belonged

A visit to Scapa Flow by the widow of the U-Boat commander who sank the Royal Oak. This photograph has just come to light of crew members of the U-47 and their wives at Scapa Flow. Third from right is Frau Prien and, fourth and fifth from right, Herbert Hermann and his Scottish wife, Ina.

The engine room of a U-boat

Life below: taking a break on a U-boat

Prien on 20th February 1941. Note how the strain of a year and a half of continual warfare has aged him. Less than a month later, he and U-47 would be lost in an attack on Convoy OB-293

The Royal Navy at its mightiest: the 2nd
Battle Squadron seen from beneath the
15-inch guns of HMS Royal Oak

Chapter 5

THE ROLL CALL OF THE *ROYAL OAK*

In total 833 lives were lost after HMS *Royal Oak* was sunk in 1939 and all are included in a final roll-call available for all to see in St Magnus Cathedral, Kirkwall, Orkney, and at the Scapa Flow Visitor Centre and Museum, Lyness, Orkney.

Abbott, S.E.
Ackerman, A.G.
Adams, W.P.
Agnew, C.W.
Alberry, J.
Allen, A.F.
Allen, P.L.
Amos, E.J.
Anderson, E.
Anderson, H.L.
Anderson, R.F.
Anderson, W.B.
Anderson, W.T.
Andrews, E.H.
Andrews, G.C.
Andrews, W.E.
Annell, F.W.
Armfield, L.
Armitage, F.C.
Armstrong, G.H.
Amo, R.
Ashby, K.

Ashwin, A.W.
Atherton, J.
Atherton, N.
Atkinson, J.
Atkinson, T.E.
Attard, F.
Attard, L.
Attfield, H.G.
Azzopardi, A.

Baigent, G.H.
Bailey, C.W.
Bailey, E.R.
Bain, R.
Baker, A.E.
Baker, W.G.M.
Baldwin, A.S.
Ball, H.E.
Barber, A.S.
Barber, F.
Bargery, A.E.
Barker, E.H.

Barnes-Moss, H.W.
Barnfather, R.N.
Bartlett, A.
Bartolo, J.
Bealing, F.C.
Beange, J.
Beddall, H.
Bedwell, H.
Beechey, A.C.
Beer, A.E.
Bell, R.W.
Bendall, R.F.J.
Bennett, W.
Benney, C.E.
Beswick, H.W.J.
Betts, H.J.
Betts, W.T.
Billyard, N.
Binnington, A.
Binns, F.B.
Binsley, G.F.
Birtchnell, C.E.

Black, J.
Blackborough, J.W.
Blagrove, H.E.C.
Blenkiron, N.
Blood, S.
Blyth, H.B.
Boening, J.
Bold, P.W.
Bonello, S.
Bonner,W.C.
Borland, D.A.
Bottomley, R.J.
Bowden, R.C.
Bowen, J.
Bowhay, W.J.R.
Boyd, T.A.
Boyes, L.S.
Boyle, W.
Brading, C.E.
Bradwick, A.H.
Bramley, R.J.
Branch, H.
Bridges, J.G.C.
Bright, H.
Brightman, G.R.
Briscoe, E.
Britton, T.F.
Brookin, J.F.
Broughton, A.E.
Brown, A.G.
Brown, D.A.J.
Brown, H.
Brown, H.W.
Brown, J.
Brymer, E.A.
Buckett, S.V.
Bucknall, A.G.
Budge, J.
Bull, A.N.
Burden, A.E.
Burnham, P.
Burns, A.

Burns, J.E.
Burrows, R.W.
Burt, E.H.
Burtenshaw, C.H.
Burton, J.W.
Butler, A.A.
Butler, A.E.
Butler, A.E.
Bydawell, L.R.J.

Cachia, J.
Cairns, J.
Campbell, C.H.
Campbell, D.
Campsie, C.
Cannon, R.J.
Capel, C.W.
Card, A.R.W.
Carnegie, A.K.
Carpenter, E.G.
Carr, F.C.
Carter, G.W.
Carter, J.
Carter, R.W.H.
Carter, W.F.
Cartwright, W.
Cass, L. Cast, R.I.
Chadwick, J.C.
Chadwick, T.
Chalk, R.G.
Challenger, A.L.
Chappell, W.G.
Cheesley, W.H.G.
Chesman, W.E.
Chick, A.
Church, O.
Clacher, W.H.
Clackson, R.G.
Clark, A.H.
Clark, A.J.
Clark, F.H.
Clark, J.

Clark, R.L.W.
Clark, F.H.
Clarke, R.E.
Clements, E.F.J.
Clementson, J.
Cloute, E.C.
Cock, C.H.
Coffin, L.J.
Colbourne, F.E.
Colbourne, J.W.F.
Colbran, P.B.
Coleman, E.W.
Coleman, J.A.
Coleman, M.G.N.
Collins, G.A.
Collins, R.
Comber, A.E.B.
Connor, F.
Connor, R.J.
Conroy, F.
Cook, G.J.
Cooke, F.A.
Cooper, L.L.
Cooper, N.
Cope, J.R.
Coreshi, E.
Cornelious, K.T.
Cornelius, H.J.
Cornish, C.F.
Cousins, H.J.
Cox, E.
Cragg, W.
Craven, A.
Cree, J.D.B.
Crockett, J.S.
Crofts, E.A.
Cross, E.V.A.
Crosswell, W.H.
Cumbes, R.W.
Cumming, L.T.J.
Cummings, H.
Cunningham, E.W.

Curtin, C.
Curtis, H.H.W.
Cutler, J.A.

Daniels, G.
Darnell, G.T.
Daughtrey, A.
Davey, C.B.
Davie, R.C.
Davies, H.R.
Davies, M.C.
Davis, J.F.
Davis, R.E.
Daysh, A.
Deacon, W.J.
Dear, A.J.
Deighton, E.C.
Derbyshire, R.
Derry, J.O.H.
Diaper, S.T.
Dickie, W.A.
Doe, S.P.
Doggett, I.E.
Dowding, P.W.G.
Downes, A.F.
Draper, B.H.
Druce, A.
Duncalf, T.
Dunk, C.A.
Dunk, W.W.
Dyer, H.

Eade, J.H.
Easton, F.
Ede, F.
Edwards, A.
Edwards, J.F.
Edwards, R.G.
Edwards, W.R.A.
Efemey, R.B.
Elliott, R.
Eltringham, N.

Emery, A.
Emery, F.C.
Evans, B.
Evans, J.E.
Eyers, C.E.

Fairbrother, J.W.
Farr, E.W.
Farrell, R.
Fenn, T.R.P.
Finlay, M.B.
Fisher, B.L.
Fisher, J.B.
Fitch, C.E.
Flogwell, A.E.
Flounders, A.
Ford, W.J.
Forsey, H.S.
Foster, D.C.
Foster, G.W.
Flouger, A.
Fowler, J.W.
Foyle, A.A.
Francis, H.A.
Franckeiss, E.L.
French, C.
Fuller, C.W.
Furbear, T.G.
Furby, E.A.
Furlong, J.
Furnell, L.T.

Gallagher, J.W.
Gibbons, J.A.
Gibson, G.
Gibson, S.J.
Gile, W.H.
Gill, G.E.
Gill, H.W.
Gillis, G.W.
Glasspool, H.
Godley, S.G.

Godwin, T.G.
Godwin, W.
Golding, A.
Goodyear, J.C.
Goorlay, J.R.G.
Gorsuch, E.D.
Gough, E.J.
Gough, T.E.
Gowan, J.D.
Grace, V.M.
Graham, G.M.
Graham, P.W.C.
Graham, S.
Graham-Brown, J.L.T.
Gray, A.
Gray, E.
Gray, H.W.
Grech, J.
Green, F.
Green, F.A.
Green, R.
Greenwood, L,
Griffin, H.
Griffiths, E.J.
Griffiths, J.R.
Grindey, A.E.
Grogan, J.
Giusti, I.
Gutteridge, R.G.N.
Guy, R.

Hales, J.
Hall, H.J.
Hall, J.
Hall, K.E.
Hall, W.R.
Hamblin, G.A.
Hammond, J.S.
Hammond, W.L.
Hance, T.R.
Harkin, P.R.
Harle, G.

Harley, J.A.H.
Harper, R.R.J.
Harris, G.J.
Harris, K.J.
Harris, N.H.
Harris, P.W.
Hawkins, K.R.J.
Hawkins, W.J.
Hayes, T.
Hayward, J.G.
Heather, C.W.
Helmore, W.L.
Hemestretch, C.W.
Hemsley, C.F.
Henstridge, C.
Heslop, C.
Hicks, A.E.
Higgins, J.J.
Higgs, H.H.
Highfield, J.E.
Hill, A.
Hill, D.
Hill, D.
Hill, E.F.
Hill, S.
Hillier, C.W.
Hingston, E.
Hiscock, F.J.
Hixson, H.H.
Hocking, J.R.
Hodgson, A.R.
Hodgson, J.S.
Hodson, F.H.J.
Holland, C.
Holyoak, E.
Hotton, L.W.T.
Hudson, J.C.
Huggins, H.S.
Hughes, F.E.
Hughes, T.
Hughes-Rowlands, R.
Hull, E.C.

Hull, R.G.
Humber, J.F.
Hunt, A.V.
Hunt, E.G.
Hunter, F.
Hunter, J.
Hurst, F.
Huscroft, R.W.
Hussey-Yeo, A.J.
Hutchcocks, T.
Hyde, A.J.
Hyde, G.M.

Ing, R.,

Jack, J.D.
Jackman, J.J.
Jackson, L.T.D.
Jackson, T.W.
Jacobs, W.A.C.
Jago, L.
James, L.J.
James, R.
James, V.L.
Jay, V.G.U.
Jelley, L.J.
Jenkins, E.J.A.
Jenkins, T.S.
Jennings, R.E.
Jewell, A.
Jewer, S.A.
Jobson, J,B.
Johns, P.H.M.
Johnson, F.W.P.
Johnson, T.W.
Johnston, A.J.
Jones, C.E.
Jones, H.
Jones, H.G.
Jones, S.
Jones, T.J.
Jordon, F.

Jordon, H.D.
Judge, P.R.

Kane, R.C.
Kearey, A.
Keel, J.
Keel, W.
Kemp, L.H.
Kempster, A.
Kennedy, R.H.
Kennedy, W.T.
Kennett, E.H.
Kent, H.A.J.
Kenworthy, J.
Kersey, H.A.
Kidby, W.F.
King, C.E.M.
King, F.W.
King, W.L.
Kirkby, D.E.
Knight, G.E.W.,

Laban, K.G.
Lardner, F.M.
Lawrence, J.E.
Leach, E.C.
Lenz, B.H.
Lester, R.
Lewis, C.E.
Lewis, D.J.
Liddell, R.
Lilley, H.G.
Liptrot, F.
Lister, H.G.
Littlejohn, J.B.M.
Lloyd, R.G.
Lloyds, S.R.
Loats, T.R.
Lock, L.F.
Lockwood, W.
Logan, F.
Long, A.

Lowery, D.
Lynch, H.C.
Lyons, J.

MacAngus, D.
McArthur, A.
McBain, D.
McBrown, R.S.
MacDermott, A.D.
McDonald, A.
MacGibbon, T.H.
McGregor, G.D.
McGregor, R.
McLaren, W.
McLennan, A.J.
Mackinnon, D.
McMilland, G.A.
McPherson,
MacReady, J.A.
McTaggart, D.

Magion, J.P.
Maher, C.
Malyon, S.H.
Mamo, F.
Manning, J.
Mansfield, W.H.
Manwaring, D.
Manwaring, W.
Marlow, A.J.
Marsh, J.W.
Marsh, O.F.
Marshall, F.
Martin, E.J.
Martin, H.J.
Martin, L.G.
Matfield, A.H.
Mather, G.
Matthews, F.H.
Matthews-Sheen, T.
Meaden, F.E.B.
Medley, B.

Mellor, S.
Merifield, W.J.
Middleton, A.F.C.
Milborn, P.
Miles, A.
Miles, A.W.S.
Miles, E.H.
Miles, P.
Milford, A.E.
Miller, A.E.
Miller, J.H.
Milligan, J.M.
Millis, R.
Millmore, F.
Milness, R.W.
Minns, F.A.
Mirfin, G.D.
Mitchell, J.H.
Mitchell, J.S.
Moar, J.W.
Moffat, J.B.
Mooney, P.
Moore, I.
Moore, J.E.
Moore, L.G.
Moore, W.J.
Morey, F.J.M.
Morris, C.H.
Morrison, J.
Morrison, J.
Morse, D.L.G.
Moses, L.D.
Mosley, J.H.
Mould, R.W.
Mountain, F.
Mountford, H.C.L.
Moylan, T.
Mullen, T.G.
Mullin, C.T.
Munro, J.
Murphy, P.
Murphy, T.

Murray, W.R.
Mutlow, L.C.
Myers, G.E.

Naisby, T.F.
Needham, E.
Newman, W.H.
Newnham, E.
Newnham, K.G.
Newsham, H.
Newsome, G.
Niblett, C.H.
Nichol, G.
Nicholls, A.H.
Nicholson, W.D.
Nixon, H.
Nuttall, F.R.M.

O'Brien, A.E.
O'Shea, M.
Offer, C.H.
Ogden, G.R.
Osborne, T.G.
Overton, J.J.
Oxley, G.R.
Oxley, H.

Paice, H.F.
Palfreyman, J.
Palmer, C.J.
Palmer, G.J.
Pape, E.W.A.S.
Park, A.A.
Parker, A.G.
Parker, J.
Parker, R.T.
Parkinson, G.H.
Parr, W.A.
Parrish, W.H.
Parry, G.J.
Parsons, G.E.
Partlett, E.G.

Parch, D.G.
Paterson, W.D.
Patterson, N.M.
Paul, L.W.C.
Pearson, A.R.
Pennel, J.A.
Pennycord, J.A.
Percy, K.B.
Perkins, E.E.G.
Perkins, R.J.
Perry, D.W.
Pesci, E.
Peters, E.R.
Peters, G.
Phelps, C.E.
Phipps, C.P.
Pickard, S.E.
Piddington, P.G.
Pierson, A.J.
Pike, A.C.
Pilkington, H.
Pine, B.
Pitkin, F.
Pollard, G.E.
Pollard, G.R.
Pope, G.A.
Porter, E.R.
Porter, H.W.
Porter, J.S.
Potter, A.
Potter, S.
Pottle, R.V.T.
Poulter, R.
Powell, A.
Powell, D.W.
Powles, W.
Pragnell, S.L.
Pratt, C.
Preston, F.H.
Priest, W.C.H.
Priestley, A.J.
Prince, G.A.

Pryor, R.A.
Puddy, R.G.
Pye, P.K.

Quantrell, O.
Quigley, A.
Quinn, H.
Quinney, G.

Radford, R.
Raine, G.H.
Ramsay, W.D.
Rann, F.
Razey, A.E.
Read, R.V.
Reed, W.G.F.
Reid, D.
Restell, A.E.
Reynolds, D.A.
Richards, W.M.
Ridsdale, G.H.
Riley, J.
Ritchie, R.C.
Roberts, A.
Roberts, F.W.
Roberts, T.O.
Robertson, N.G.
Robertson, R.U.
Robins, C.F.
Rollo, D.
Roper, D.
Ross, G.I.McL.
Ross, T.W.
Roupell, M.P.
Rouse, P.
Rowll, A.W.
Roxborough, T.
Royal, W.D.
Ruck, W.S.
Russell, W.F.E.
Rustell, S.
Rutherford, J.J.

Rutter, W.
Ryall, M.G.
Ryan, M.J.
Ryan, W.D.,

Sa-ib-a, L.
Sandford, F.W.G.
Sandham, G.M.
Savage, C.H.
Savage, W.J.B.
Scarlett, A.
Schiavone, E.
Schofield, R.
Scott, W.
Searle, J.G.
Seaton, E.F.
Seeley, E.J.
Senlor, F.
Sharp, R.
Shaw, S.
Shepherd, G.
Sheppard, E.W.
Sheriff, J.G.
Shorrock, K.W.
Short, W.
Sibley, A.
Sibley, C.
Simmons, J.S.
Simmons, O.A.J.
Simpson, G.R.
Simpson, J.R.
Simpson, R.H.
Simpson, S.
Sinclair, W.
Slade, S.J.
Slawson, W.
Small, W.
Smith, C.J.
Smith, D.E.
Smith, D.H.
Smith, G.
Smith, G. W.

Smith, H.
Smith, J.A.
Smith, R.
Snellock, R.A.
Sorley, J.N.
Spalding, R.F.J.
Sparrow, L.
Spelman, D.B.T.
Spence, W.G.
Spencer, A.K.
Spencer, C.J.
Spencer, H.
Spencer, W.H.
Spicer, H.H.
Squires, L.G.
Stables, G.
Stambridge, H.W.
Standen, G.H.
Stanley, C.J.
Stannard, W.E.
Steele, C.A.
Steele, R.F.
Stemp, N.H.
Stephens, H.
Stephens, M.W.
Stephenson, J.G.
Stevens, H.J.
Stevenson, E.J.
Stevenson, J.
Stewart, D.C.C.
Stewart, H.
Stokes, H.J.
Stokes, J.L.
Stone, W.F.
Strickley, H.F.
Summersby, F.
Sumner, P.
Sutherland, H.J.

Talbot, F.G.
Tanner, B.C.
Targett, T.H.

Taylor, D.
Taylor, E.G.
Taylor, R.J.
Taylor, S.
Taylor, W.M.
Tee, J.G.
Tester, C.A.
Thirkell, R.
Thomas, R.A.
Thompson, J.
Thompson, R.
Thompson, R.
Thomson, J.
Thorne, L.F.
Thwaites, R.W.
Tidey, A.E.
Tiplady, T.
Todd, G.
Touse, J.W.
Townsend, T.H.
Trayfoot, A.G.
Treleaven, C.N.E.
Trenholm, T.W.
Trevett, E.M.
Trussler, L.G.
Tuckwood, W.S.
Turner, S.V.
Tutton, R.E.

Usmar, H.W.B.

Vass, B.
Vass, D.
Vass, H.
Vine, J.

Wadsworth, A.H.
Wakefield, H.
Walker, C.
Walker, D.
Walker, E.
Walker, F.

Wallace, A.J.
Walton, J.H.
Ward, G.
Ward, G.
Ward, R.D.
Warner, L.J.
Warriner, J.B.
Waterfield, W.A.
Waterman, V.P.
Watkins, S.M.
Watson, G.
Watson, J.
Watson, R.H.
Watson, W.
Watts, H.C.
Weatherburn, S.
Webb, D.H.
Webb, R.S.
Weller, H.A.
West, D.
Westbrook, P.E.
Westell, S.A.
Western, R.
Westnutt, E.
Wheeler, E.
White, E.
White, G.
White, H.J.W.
White, J.
White, J.
White, W.R.
Whitmore, E.
Wittaker, W.J.
Wiggins, L.W.
Wilcock, E.A.
Wilkins, J.P.
Wilkinson, J.
Willard, L.F.
Willeter, J.E.
William, J.
Williams, C.
Williams, F.M.

Williams, G.A.

Williams, J.

Wilmington, F.H.

Wilmot, D.G.

Wilshaw, J.T.

Wilshire, E.

Wilson, A.

Wilson, A.R.

Wilson, G.R.

Wilson, R.

Wilson, R.V.

Wilson, S.V.M.

Wood, J.

Wood, R.G.P.

Wood, S.

Wood, W.J.

Woodcock, A.G.

Woodford, G.

Woolgar, D.R.

Wormald, J.L.

Wren, V.G.

Wright, F.E.

Wright, W.G.

Xureb, J.

Yates, J.A.

Zahra, J.

Newspaper cuttings. Reproduced with the kind permission of The Daily Telegraph.

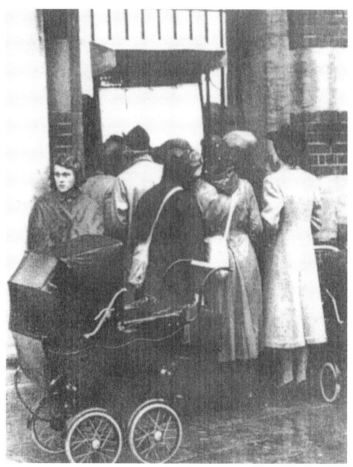

The families of those serving on HMS Royal Oak hunt for names on the list of survivors

Survivors

Adams, R.L.
Affleck-Graves, G.
Alford, E.C.
Allridge, A.
Amer, A.
Anderson, R.
Andrews, G.R.
Anslow, B.J.
Aplin, W.H.
Archer, L.
Arnell, G.R.
Ashley, R.
Askham, R.W.
Atmeare, G.W.C.
Atter, J.
Ayles, V.L.T.

Babb, A.J.
Baker, G.R.
Baker, R.
Balch, H.,C.
Ball, C.W.
Bardsell, W.J.
Barrett, W.
Bateman, R.H.
Batterbury, W.G.
Belben, D.
Bell, I.
Bendell, R.
Benn, W.G.
Benton, M.H.
Bevis, A.H.
Bignell, C.S.
Billingham, J.P.

Birch, R.G.
Bish, H.
Bishop, T.G.
Blackmor, D.
Blake, M.
Blowers, A.F.
Blundell, T.W.A.
Bond, A.
Booth, G.H.
Borthwick, S.
Bowes, M.
Boxall, E.A.
Breen, J.
Brierley, A.
Brigden, W.S.
Britt, E.R.
Brocker, E.R.A.
Bromyard, J.
Brooke, F.
Brown, A.D.
Brown, J.
Bryan, L.
Bryant, J.E.
Bulley, F.J.
Burnside, J.
Burton, R.D.
Butcher, N.

Caldwell, D.
Camenzuli, A.
Campbell, W.M.
Cartwright, C.P.
Casey, W.P.
Chalder, J.

Chalker, A.
Chatfield, A.G.
Childs, G.J.
Childs, L.
Chown, W.E.
Clarke, E.
Clarke, W.H.
Clayton, J.W.J.
Clayton, K.B.
Clements, F.S.
Cleverly, H.P.
Coade, J.A.
Coady, J.
Cole, S.
Collier, J.
Combes, F.S.
Combes, P.W.C.
Connelly, M.
Connor, R.
Conway, K.G.
Cook, D.S.
Cook, F.N.
Cook, G.F.
Cook, S.H.
Coombes, J.J.
Coote, A.G.
Coulson, T.S.
Cowen, W.
Cox, H.P.T.
Crichton, [?]
Cripps, W.A.
Cross, F.
Crowther, W.H.
Cruse, V.

Cundall, J.R.
Cutler, F.

Dall, F.O'N.
Davey, M.F.
Davidson, K.E.
Davies, N.T.
Davis, E.E.
Dawson, S.R.
Densham, E.D.
Devlyn, J.C.
Dewey, K.G.
Dommett, E.
Dove, G.E.
Dowling, H.V.
Drew, T.R.
Duncan, H.
Dunne, W.A.
Dunstone, G.

Edmunds, R.
Edwards, W.A.
Ellis, G.
Elmes, A.
Evans, E.A.
Evans, S.,

Fairney, E.H.
Farley, A.J.
Farmer, H.
Farquhar, J.
Ferrugi, J.
Fiddler, E.J.
Figg, J.
Finlaysson, R.H.
Finley, N.
Fisher, G.W.
Fleming, E.
Fletcher, O.L.
Forder, K.B.
Fordham, A.L.
Fossey, W.J.

Foster, T.J.
Fox, W.T.J.
Freer, T.F.
Frost, A.V.

Gardiner, R.H.
Gattrell, F.M.
Gearing, A.
Gibbs, A.R.F.
Gibson, W.
Gilmore, E.J.
Goodland, J.R.
Goodson, H.
Grant, N.W.
Green, Reginald C.
Green, Ronald C.
Gregory, R.A.V.
Grove, R.C.,

Haig, J.D.
Haigh, S.W.
Halford, J.L.
Hall, C.J.
Hall, J.
Hall, R.E.A.
Hancox, W.
Hanharan, F.
Harboard, R.V.
Harding, W.E.
Harks, F.L.
Harland, T.
Harmer, A.
Harrington, K.
Harris, D.T.
Harris, E.
Harris, E.J.
Harrison, G.S.
Hart, D.J.
Hartley, J.A.
Harty, J.
Hasler, J.E.
Hastings, A.

Hawes, B.
Hayhow, R.
Head, S.P.
Hearn, J.V.
Hickman, K.
Hickmore, A.
Higgins, P.
Hilkin, B.H.
Hinde, N.L.
Hine, C.
Hine, N.J.
Hobbs, F.J.C.
Holligan, M.
Hollis, J.E.
Hoskins, A.J.
Howard, A.R.
Howe, H.
Howell, R.S.
Hughlock, W.
Humby, W.E.
Hutchings, W.K.
Hutchinson, Wm.

Ingpen, J.P.
Ings, A.G.
Instance, H.J.

Jackson, R.E.
Jacobs, E.
Johnston, H.R.
Jones, R.S.
Jones, T.H.
Jordan, A.R.
Judge, F.G.

Keen, B.B.
Kelly, H.A.G.
Kenny, R.J.
Kerr, J.R.
Kersely [?]
Ketcher, A.D.
Kichener, A.D.

Knott, A.H.

Lakin, T.H.
Langlands, G.A.
Lawrence, A.
Lawrence, W.A.
Lazell, N.
Leadlay, K.R.S.
Lee, J.H.
Lees, R.
Lettin, J.T.
Lidget, E.E.
Lipscombe, C.G.
Lloyd, D.J.
Lockyear, G.L.J.
Lucking, C.J.
Lutman, H.J.

McCabe, C.B.
McCarthy, F.
McLaverty, J.
MacLean, Q.G.S.
Maggs, G.J.
Main, H.W.
Makin, J.H.
Mallis, L.
Marchant, V.
Marsh, W.A.
Martin, F.A.
Martin, R.
Masters, D.W.
Mawson, M.G.H.
Mead, J.N.
Melrose, J.R.
Merrick, T.
Miles, R.S.
Milligan, L.W.
Mitchell, W.C.
Moore, E.A.
Moppeti, A.J.
Morley, R.
Morris, P.J.

Murray, J.
Murrin, C.W.T.

Neville, P.
Newton, D.
Nichols, R.F.
Noble, T.A.,

O'Bryne, D.P.
O'Leary, J.D.F.
Orges, R.H.
Owens, P.H.
Owens, W.

Pagett, I.H.
Palmer, W.G.
Parham, G.E.T.
Patterson, A.
Pattison, H.
Payton, J.A.
Pearman, A.H.
Peay, J.F.
Phillips, W.G.
Pipes, H.
Pirie, R.P.
Pitcher, A.T.
Pither, H.W.
Pocock, H.E.
Poling, G.R.
Ope, R.
Potter, T.W.
Potts, H.H.
Pouttner, C.S.
Pritchard, B.W.
Protheroe, G.
Prowse, G.

Radford, J.A.
Randall, E.
Randell, H.
Ransome, F.
Redman, A.

Renshaw, J.W.
Richard, P.
Riley, C.H.
Ritchie, G.L.
Roberts, G.O.
Roberts, L.H.
Robertson, N.C.
Rockingham, N.W.
Rose, P.
Ross, James
Ross, John
Rowland, E.A.
Rowlands, S.
Saltmarch, S.
Sammit, E.
Sandifer, W.E.
Scarff, A.W.
Sclater, C.E.L.
Scott, E.L.
Scovell, E.W.
Seaburn-May, R.M.
Seymour, A.E.
Seymour, A.M.
Sheldrick, D.W.V.
Sherwood, J.
Shuter, J.W.D.
Sidley, W.F.
Sims, F.G.
Skilling, M.
Smart, W.H.
Smith, A.
Smith, E.
Smith, G.
Smith, G.A.
Smith, J.H.
Smith, W.
Smithalls, J.K.
Soal, L.
Spituary, P.
Spurling, W.G.
Stares, G.R.
Stephen, G.P.

Stevens, T.B.

Stewart, E.S.

Stimson, R.F.

Storar, T.R.

Sturdee, P.D.

Sylvester, R.G.

Symes-Thompson,M.F.J.

Symonds, H,G.

Tate, W.

Taylor, T.W.R.

Terry, A.H.

Terry, P.

Thackeray, N.E.

Thompson, J.F.P.

Thompson, N.E.

Thompson, S.W.H.

Thompson, V.R.

Throssell, W.H.

Tily, R.

Timms, J.

Toop, K.H.

Trewinnard, G.

Tunnicliff, L.H.

Turner, R.A.

Turvey, A.R.

Tutton, A.E.

Upham, E.F.

Vennel, George F.

Vincent, J.T.E.,

Wadham, H.F.

Ward, D.H.

Ward, M.R.F.

Ward, R.M.

Warren, J.G.

Watten, R.P.

Weare, W.T.

Weir, W.

Welch, J.

Wernham, H.J.

Westcott, C.

Wheatland, A.J.

Wheeler, D.R.

Whincup, R.W.

Whitbread, E.

White, F.

White, G.R.

White, P.A.

Whitehouse, G.

Whitlock, J.T.

Wilkinson, A.P.

Williams, F.

Williams, G.B.

Williams, M.

Willoughby, K.H.

Wilson, C.J.

Wilson, R.E.

Wiltshire, F.W.

Winterbottom, G.E.

Wisden, T.F.

Wood, K.J.J.

Wood, R.H.

Wood, S.R.

Woodnutt, W.E.

Woods, H.J.

Woods, H.J.C.

Woods, J.W.

Woolnough, G.H.

Wright, H.

Zarb, P.

An artist's impression of the wreck of HMS Royal Oak. The deck now lies at approximately 45 degrees to the sea bed and most of the superstructure is crushed beneath the upturned hull

Original marker buoy. Land was only 1000 yards away but few
survivors reached its safety. The plaque on the original marker buoy
reads: 'This marks the wreck of HMS Royal Oak and the grave of her
crew. Respect their resting place. Unauthorised diving prohibited.'
Reproduced with kind permission of Charles Tait, St. Ola, Orkney

The modern buoy that now marks the Royal Oak's final resting place

Chapter 6

Rescue

The entire transport of personnel, of food supply and of mail to British warships at anchor was carried out by drifters, which in peacetime were simple fishing boats. Manned by their hardy fishermen crews, these small craft acted in all weathers as ferries, water carriers, target-towing vessels and as hospital boats to the Royal Navy. Many of the drifter men were awarded decorations for bravery, including the Victoria Cross.

One well-known drifter skipper was 40 year old John Gatt from Rosehearty on the North-East coast of Scotland. He won a DSC for rescuing 386 survivors from the torpedoed *Royal Oak*. He treasured even more than his DSC a silver watch presented to him by the parents and friends of the men he saved.

Johnnie Duthie, a crew member on John Gatt's boat, never thought that he would be in the company of men with so much courage in the face of peril on the sea. They all had great faith and that is what kept them going; their strength that night was beyond human endurance. They gave their all, and asked for nothing. They all worked together that night as a team, picking men out of the water, their strength ebbing all the time.

Their Skipper, John Gatt , never lost his great courage all through that night in October 1939, but, as the long dawn came, there was a deadly silence in Scapa Flow, because over 800 men were still missing and no longer had any chance of survival. By the time dawn broke, they were now just six men, confused and tired, but, amidst the sorrow that so many brave sailors had lost their lives, they had the joy of knowing that they had rescued 360 men from a watery grave.

Luckily for the drifter, *Daisy II* and her crew, they had moored along the port side of the *Royal Oak* and were thus clear of the initial devastating explosions. Johnnie Duthie recalled that they had gone to bed, only to be awakened by a massive explosion. They went up on deck and a Naval Officer from the battleship asked what was happening. Nobody seemed to know, but there was some speculation that the explosion had been made by a bomb dropped from a German aircraft which had escaped before the shore batteries could open fire.

For some reason, Johnnie Duthie didn't go back to bed, although the other members of the crew did. But they were to get little sleep, for there was another horrendous explosion around six to eight minutes after the first one. After the second explosion, they stood with their skipper on the deck and watched the great battleship roll over within six minutes of being torpedoed and all around men were crying for help.

At this point, they had to fight to save their own boat as the mighty battleship began to keel over lifting the drifter by her mooring ropes out of the sea. The *Daisy II* was held by ropes from stern and bow to the battleship's port side. The drifter was in imminent danger of going under. When the crew saw what was happening, they ran forward and cut the rope at the stern and immediately the *Daisy II* dropped away from the side of the *Royal Oak* and clear of the rapidly submerging battleship.

There were so many acts of bravery that night. There was no time to think, everything happened so quickly and with little or no warning, leaving everyone in a state of shock. Things were done because they had to be done

Regardless of their own safety, the entire crew of *Daisy II* began to pluck their unfortunate comrades from this turbulent, frothing pit of hell. The task of picking survivors out of the dark, murky water became increasingly difficult. Furnace oil from the battleship was escaping into the sea and, as the twisted metal hurtled downwards to the ocean bed, the crude black mass floated continually upwards, flooding the surface with a thick greasy film and creating havoc among the struggling survivors. After the final flame was swallowed up and the sea engulfed the last lingering piece of wreckage, the night sky plunged Scapa Flow into a deathly darkness.

Daisy II was amidst hundreds of sailors shouting for help and deliverance from their plight. Hauling the sailors up onto the gas-lit drifter became a soul-destroying job – for all were a pitiful sight. Many were wounded and badly burned. One sailor called out to them and said that he could not see as oil was in his eyes. Although they tried to get hold of him, he kept swimming further into the darkness still crying for help. Another rescued sailor with pluck and determination insisted that he re-enter the murky depths again and again to pull his shipmates clear of the deadly furnace oil. A doctor serving on board HMS *Royal Oak* was lifted onto the drifter and he tirelessly treated his injured patients. Rear Admiral Blagrove, after refusing a lifebuoy offered to him by a crew member of *Daisy II*, said, "I must look after my men." He was never seen again.

Daisy II

The crew of the Daisy II

John Stephen   John Gardener Johnnie Duthie

John Gatt, DSC, from Rosehearty, skipper of Daisy II

Alex Stephen   Bobbie Duthie

The strain must have been hard on the rescuers surrounded by such afflictions and the last call of those who were giving up the fight became a chilling experience. Like the sailor who, with his last breath, uttered, 'Say goodbye to my wife and children.' That is why none of the crew of *Daisy II* ever forgot the experiences they went through that night. It was a horrific experience for all involved; the mental, as well as the physical torture was to last a lifetime.

John Gatt, the Skipper, remained calm throughout, giving orders in a quiet, controlled voice and manoeuvring the drifter easily amongst the battleship's survivors, aiding the crew to bring the drowning sailors on board. The last survivors they took aboard were a terrible sight for them all. Their skin hung in shreds down their arms, they all had a lost look in their eyes and sometimes when they were being hauled on to the drifter they often shouted, 'Don't touch me.'

Without *Daisy II*, her skipper John Gatt and his crew, many more would have died in one of the worst tragedies in British naval history.

Their courage must never be forgotten.

Veritas

Sixty nine years have gone by since the infamous sinking of the battleship *Royal Oak*. Stories as yet unpublished still surface from many sources.

Do we really know the truth even today as to what did happen at Scapa Flow on that fateful night of 14th October 1939?

I received a letter from Mr D. Wathen, Tobermory, Isle of Mull, in 2005. He says that in the early 1960s he was part of a four man team sent by the National Farmers Union Scotland to investigate the farming problem which existed on Orkney at that time.

He was billeted with a family who crofted land near to the dark 600 feet cliffs where many of the crew of the *Royal Oak,* to use his words, 'finished up', after having swum from the stricken battleship one and a half miles away. He goes on to say that the crofter, his family and his neighbours wanted to go down the cliff by torchlight to rescue possible survivors but the police and coastguard stopped them. The saddest aspect of this whole affair he says was that the locals knew a path down the cliff and could have guided some of the sailors to safety. Almost all perished at the foot of the cliffs on that dreadful night.

The loss was of 24 officers and 809 men, some of whom according to the statement made in his letter did not die on the battleship, but at the foot of the cliffs.

How could this be? Did anyone really know in all the confusion just how many men were down there? As to my knowledge there are only 26 members of the crew buried on land – in the Royal Navy Cemetery on the Island of Hoy, one officer, my uncle Commander Ralph Lennox Woodrow-Clark and 25 other ranks. It begs the question therefore, just how many crew members were alive, and just how many died at the cliff face. Are any other members of the crew buried elsewhere on Orkney, or were the deceased returned to their loved ones for burial, or were they left at the foot of those cliffs to be swallowed up by the sea and never retrieved?

The letter in question was written on 14th April 2005. The content was controversial to say the least.

On 15th May 2006 I began the journey to Mull from my home in Manchester, travelling to Glasgow and onward to Oban to board the ferry to Craignure, Mull, then by coach travelling north across the island to my final destination at Tobermory.

On the morning of the 16th I finally met 'the man behind the letter', at his home on the island. He was of small stature, with angular features, in his mid seventies, extremely articulate and of a friendly disposition.

He was born in 1928 in Weisbaden, the son of a serving cavalry officer. Educated at Marlborough College, Wiltshire, he entered the Royal Navy in 1945. After leaving the Navy he went to agricultural college, with a view to pursuing a career in farming.

He was on two occasions adopted as a parliamentary candidate for Inverness by the Conservative Party, on the second occasion coming second to Russell Johnston, the Liberal. He stands by everything he says in his letter and is adamant that the Orcadians with whom he was billeted were not confusing the issue of HMS *Hampshire* in World War I with that of HMS *Royal Oak* in World War II.

Recent research has revealed that the battleship *Royal Oak* was not declared an official war grave until some time after her sinking. The Admiralty did consider a survey of the sunken ship to assess the possibility of salvage, but due to massive public outcry they abandoned the idea.

The Navy reacted very quickly to the tragedy of 14th October 1939 and the following day nets were spread over the battleship to contain any bodies which otherwise would have been carried away and probably never recovered. At that time in Scapa Flow, prior to the completion of the Churchill Barriers, there was a severe undertow tidal race. Although we are now aware that 833 officers and crew members perished, according to information to hand some of them did not die within the battleship itself but drowned in the bitingly cold oil-covered waters of Scapa Flow. Divers did go down to inspect the wreck and did see entombed bodies. It stretches credulity to assume that 817 officers and crew members actually went down to the sea bed within the battleship. Just how many did get off to swim to shore, any shore, will never be known, apart from those lucky ones who were rescued by the drifter *Daisy II*. It is conceivable to believe that many may have reached the foot of those cliffs mentioned in the letter, but the respective authorities would have deemed it to be too dangerous to attempt rescue, especially at night. No one can be sure or made accountable after all these years. The 'cruel sea' is their grave.

Twenty six bodies were recovered from the sea. Many more who possibly escaped from the ship were never seen again. Of the 833 men lost, many died inside the ship while still trying to get out.

The dead men were brought to Lyness and a number of survivors were asked to identify them. Some, with a horror of recognising friends, refused to do it. A Sergeant Booth, Royal Marines, took part – the first man he saw was a Senior Officer Engineer, almost certainly my uncle. All had died by drowning, there were no significant external wounds.

Chapter 7

FUNERAL OF THE ROYAL OAK CREW

The day of the funeral was cold and sunny. As the long lines of survivors followed a bugler and a squad of ratings with rifles at the trail up the hill above Lyness, the sun was momentarily obscured by a passing cloud. Two men in the leading file of survivors carried wreaths. Behind them followed a motley array, few of whom were properly dressed. Mostly they wore boiler suits and white gym shoes issued in the ship *Voltaire*. Many had white caps instead of black. Some were wearing clothes given to them by the crews of *Daisy II* and the *Pegasus*. As the funeral party stood with reversed arms above the grave and the bugle notes rang the Last Post over the hill the sun directly behind the ranks shone out and cast their shadows across the raw earth.

At Lyness Naval Cemetery rest the heroes from some of the most famous incidents in modern naval history – the Battle of Jutland (1916); HMS *Hampshire* sunk by a mine off Birsay (1916); explosion of the *Vanguard* off Flotta (1917); and the *Royal Oak* torpedoed in Scapa Flow.

At the end of World War I, the German High Seas Fleet was interned at Scapa Flow in Orkney, pending Armistice negotiations. On 21st June 1919, Admiral von Raeder gave the command for seventy-four German battleships, cruisers and destroyers to be scuttled rather than fall into British hands.

A memorial plaque to the men of the *Royal Oak* was erected in St Magnus Cathedral, Kirkwall, together with the ship's bell,

HMS Royal Oak funeral, October 16th, 1939

At the graveside, Lyness Naval Cemetery

Memorial plaque, St Magnus Cathedral, Kirkwall,
Orkney. Reproduced with kind permission of
Charles Tait, St. Ola, Orkney

recovered from the sea bed of Scapa Flow. The plaque was unveiled
on 14th October, 1948, the ninth anniversary of the tragedy, by Rear
Admiral W.G. Benn, who was Captain of the warship on the night
she sank, at a service attended by several other survivors. Each
day in the Cathedral, one page of a Book of Condolence is turned
in memory of the 833 officers and men who lost their lives.

In September 2003, I finally honoured my schoolboy promise to
visit my uncle's war grave and make the moving trip to a site of
sorrow, where twenty six of the dead lie.

I laid a wreath and with it a laminated message, from me, my
mother, her younger brother and other relatives, which said:

"You are still sadly missed."

Former enemies united by the same tragedy: Royal Oak sailor, Welshman Taffy Davies and Herbert Herman, crewman on the U-47, meet at a reunion in Portsmouth

The unfurling of a battle ensign on the upturned hull of the battleship Royal Oak by a Royal Navy diver on the anniversary of her sinking

When I walked into the cemetery, the sun was shining from a clear blue sky, the air was still, there was nothing to disturb the peace and tranquillity of the moment. It was an emotional experience I will never forget.

I also went to visit the site of the *Royal Oak* itself and scattered flowers on the sea in memory of all those men who went down with the ship. I felt a sense of great sadness for all those whose lives had been lost. That same evening, as the sun was setting over Scapa Flow, I flew low over the wreck site in a light aircraft and on to the Churchill barriers.

I returned to Manchester on 11th September 2003 after four unforgettable days at Scapa Flow. I related my experience to my mother who was then 93. She was delighted that, after all these

The simple wooden crosses used immediately after the funeral were later replaced by granite crosses

years, a member of the family had finally made the journey to her elder brother's last resting place. Commander Woodrow-Clark was just 33 when he was killed. He left a wife who is now deceased, and a son, Michael.

My mother Muriel Lila Turner passed away on 15th June 2007, aged 96. I made a further pilgrimage to Orkney to carry out one of her last wishes and reunite her with her brother, Commander Ralph Lennox Woodrow-Clark. Her ashes followed the route taken by the twenty six crew of the *Royal Oak* who are buried within the cemetery at Lyness on Hoy. Her ashes were taken by sea from Kirkwall to Lyness and then along the road leading to the cemetery and were buried at her brother's grave. A brother and sister torn apart by war had been reunited in death after sixty eight years.

The simple ceremony marked the first time the Commonwealth War Graves Commission had granted permission for a civilian to be buried in a military grave. My mother was a Senior Decoding Officer within the Admiralty, a factor which may have had some bearing on the Commission's decision.It was a very emotional journey and I was grateful and delighted to have been able to carry out my mother's wishes.

The author approaches the Royal Navy Cemetery on Hoy to place a tribute to his late uncle

At the site of the sinking of the mighty battleship HMS Royal Oak

Muriel Lila Turner, sister of Commander Ralph Lennox Woodrow-Clark – her ashes were buried at her brother's grave at Lyness

Chapter 8

Boys on HMS *Royal Oak*

Dr Edith Summerskill:
Asked the First Lord of the Admiralty how many boys between 14
and 18 years of age had been killed or wounded or are missing;
how many of this age are still serving in the Navy; and whether he
will agree to withdraw those who are exposed to danger and replace
them by men?

Mr Sorensen:
Asked the First Lord of the Admiralty that following the horrendous
loss of boy seamen when the *Royal Oak* was sunk, whether he will
consider the withdrawal of boys serving in His Majesty's Navy
during the war?

Mr Churchill:
There are just under 5,000 boys under 18 years of age serving at
sea, of whom 137 have been casualties. The Navy is a voluntary
service and secures a large part of its personnel by the recruitment
of continuous service boys between the ages of 15 and 16 and a
half. The consent of their parents is obtained before entry. Training
at sea is an essential part of a boy's training, and the great majority
of these boys go to sea from the age of 17 upwards. There they
perform the task appropriate to their age and training and form an
essential part of the ship's company. It is not proposed to alter a

system that has been the traditional method of providing personnel for the Navy. In future, however, the consent of the parent will be obtained if in an exceptional case the boy's training at sea will start below the age of 17.

Dr Summerskill: In view of the fact that modern Naval warfare endangers the lives of these boys, does not the Right Hon. Gentleman think that the Navy should come into line with other services, which do not send boys upon active service under the age of 18?

It should be noted that in fact after the terrible loss of boy seamen following the sinking of the *Royal Oak*, no boys under the age of 18 would again be allowed to serve on any warship during wartime, unless there were exceptional circumstances involved.

AGE 15, KILLED IN ACTION

Many boy seamen were killed in action when the Royal Oak was sunk.
The caption on this cutting from the Portsmouth News, 1939 reads:
'For three generations the Priestlys, a Portsmouth family, have had men serving in the Royal Marines. Fifteen-years-old John (above) followed in their footsteps. He became a drummer boy. . . died in the Royal Oak.'

HMS *Royal Oak* – A Boy's Story
Men swam in sea of oil

It was revealed by Mr Churchill in the House of Commons, yesterday, Wednesday 17th October 1939, that the full story of the end of *Royal Oak*, sunk at anchor by the most daring U-boat feat of the war, was told last night by a boy survivor, 18-year-old Vincent Marchant of Doncaster.

Marchant was asleep in his hammock when the first explosion rocked the ship. He ran to the upper deck to see what had happened. Twenty minutes later, there was a second explosion, followed by a third – then a fourth. By that time, the ship was listing and sinking rapidly. He remembered what had happened in the *Courageous*, his previous ship. So he stripped himself of all his clothing and, tying his safety belt around his waist, dived into the water.

Hundreds of heads

Searchlights, playing over the surface of the water, picked out hundreds of heads bobbing around in the water. Great volumes of oil started to belch up to the surface. His eyes started to smart and the faces of all the men swimming in the water turned a greasy black. He was caught in a searchlight for several minutes and saw that two of his pals were swimming alongside him. Later, however, they got cramp and went under for the last time.

Marchant, now in hospital, swam and swam in the sea of oil; he didn't know for how long but said that he must have gone about a mile and a half when he felt a rock under him. He scarcely remembered what happened after that. It was like a nightmare. He was dazed and half-conscious and just had a vague recollection of climbing up the sheer face of a cliff about 20 to 30ft high to safety. Some time later – he would say about half an hour – six men arrived with restoratives. They wrapped him in a blanket and took him to an hotel in the town nearby.

Four victims of the sinking of the battleship *Royal Oak* were buried at sea yesterday, 17th October 1939. Their bodies had been landed at Kirkwall.

These articles, first published on 18th October, 1939, are adapted with the kind permission of the *Daily Mail*

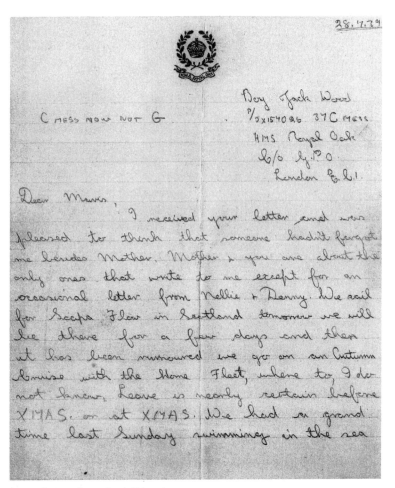

Letter home from Jack Wood

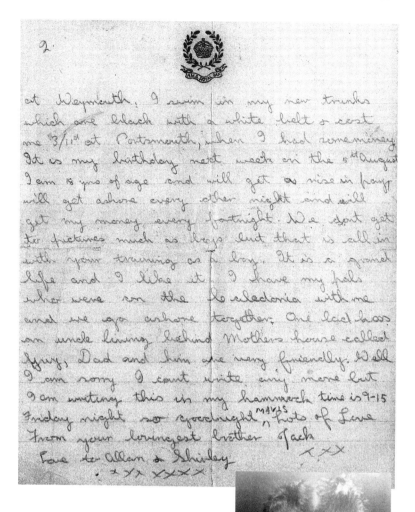

2.

at Weymouth. I swim in my new trunks which are black with a white belt & cost me 3/11d at Portsmouth, when I had some money. It is my birthday next week on the 5th August I am 18 yrs of age and will get a rise in pay, will get ashore every other night and will get my money every fortnight. We dont get to pictures much as boys but that is all in with your training as a boy. It is a grand life and I like it. I have my pals who were on the Caledonia with me and we go ashore together. One lad has an uncle living behind Mothers house called Jffry, Dad and him are very friendly. Well I am sorry I cant write any more but I am writing this in my hammock time is 9-15 Friday night so goodnight Mavis n lots of Love From your lovingest brother Jack
x x x
Love to Allan & Shirley
. x x x x x x x

Ordinary seaman Jack Wood
18 years, HMS Royal Oak

Ord/Sea J Wood
C/JX157026 11 MESS
HMS Royal Oak
C/o L/P O
London EC1

Dear Mavis,

I owe you an apology for not writing sooner but I have managed at last. Well we find ourselves at war again. I am not worrying about it but am ready to do my share. Dont worry about me I am O.K, just look after Sher and look on the bright side. Am not allowed to tell you about myself so I will close with love to all from

Your loving brother Jack
x x x

Letter home from Jack Wood
This letter was his penultimate message to home, stating that he was
happy and telling his parents not to worry. His last letter did not
reach home until his death notification which arrived the same day.

THE LOSS OF H.M.S. "ROYAL OAK"

North-West Durham's Young Victims

The loss of H.M. Royal Oak has meant darkened homes in Consett and district, and the casualties are all young men on the threshold of life.

The sympathy of the whole district goes out to the families of these sailors.

ERIC PAPE.

The death is officially announced, by Admiralty telegram, of Eric William Pape, aged 20, of 22, Queen's Road, Blackhill. He was the elder son of Mr. and Mrs. W. A. D. Pape, and in July was transferred from H.M.S. Hawkins as a leading supply assistant after approximately two years' service in the Navy. He was a pupil of Durham Johnston School and had many friends in Consett area where his father, as clerk to the local education committee, came in 1936.

JOHN STEPHENSON.

News was received at his home, 56, Constance Street, Consett, of the death of John George Stephenson, 21-year-old son of Mr. and Mrs. John Stephenson. He was a former C.I.C. employee until 3½ years ago when he joined the Navy and served on HM. Ships Blanche Verity and Coventry. At one time he was employed by Messrs. Hanson, the Consett bakers. His brother, Ernest, reports for military duty this week-end.

ARTHUR SCARLETT.

The death is announced of Arthur, only son of Mr. and Mrs. J. R. Scar-

lett, of 9, Villa Real Bungalows, Consett. He had been in the Senior Service for just twelve months and had been on H.M.S. Dunbar prior to transfer to the Royal Oak. It had been his ambition to serve in the Navy ever since leaving school and he had been employed at Derwent Colliery as an assistant onsetter, from the age of 16. On Whit-Monday he reported for duty with John Stephenson, who was one of his 'pals'. His parents had, last week, sent a parcel containing gloves and other warm things in response to his last letter in which he said he was "alright but it is cold at nights."

JACK WOOD.

From his sister, Mrs. Alan Richards, of 41, Park Road, Consett, comes the story of the last letter sent from the Royal Oak by Jack Wood, son of Mr. and Mrs. Fred Wood of 29, Finings Avenue, Langley Park. She has had two letters since the War began and the last one said "It's war again, but I am not worrying, I'm prepared to do my bit." Jack, who was 18 in August, was a native of Langley Park, where he was educated at the Council School and confirmed at All Saints. Last Easter he was home on leave to be best man at the wedding of his sister, Nellie, now Mrs. Smart, of Washington. He was training to be a gunner, and had always been keen on Navy service.

His grandmother is Mrs. E. Parry, of 10, Edith Street, Consett.

103

Ord/Sea J Wood
C/JX157026 11MES
HMS Royal Oak
c/o GPO
London E.C.
24 Sept

HIS LAST LETTER
he died 3 wks later
drowned in his ship
at Scapa Flow
R. I. P.

Dear Mavis,
I have found time to write you a short letter again and to let you know I am still as fit and happy as ever. Up to the present I have not been troubled by the war and I am not worrying. Really I am safer than you are. Goodness only knows how long this trouble will go on but I suppose it will come to an end

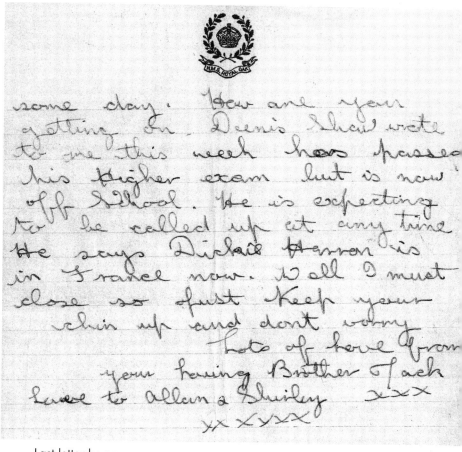

some day. How are you getting on. Denis Shaw wrote to me this week has passed his higher exam but is now off school. He is expecting to be called up at any time He says Dickie Harron is in France now. Well I must close so just keep your chin up and dont worry
Lots of love from your loving Brother Jack
Love to Allan & Shirley xxx
xxxxx

Last letter home

SON'S LETTER CAME WITH NEWS OF HIS DEATH

LANGLEY PARK LAD LOST IN ROYAL OAK

Official notification of the death in the Royal Oak disaster of their elder son, Jack, has been received by Mr. and Mrs. Fred Wood, of 29, Finings-avenue, Langley Park. He was 18.

At the same time as they received news of his death Mr. and Mrs. Wood received a letter—his last—from their son. Referring in this letter to a pet "budgie" of the family, he wrote "The bird will keep you all company and will amuse me when (underlined) I come h o m e, though this is not very certain. D o n ' t worry about me, because I am O.K. You would not think there was a war on where I am; everything is so quiet."

JACK WOOD.

Wood, an ordinary seaman, was trained on the Caledonia and was later transferred to the Royal Oak. He had lived at Langley Park from birth and on leaving school was employed in the Co-operative Laundries at Neville's Cross. Later he worked at the King's Cinema, Langley Park, but he left his employment to join the Navy. In his younger days he was a Sunday school scholar at Langley Park All Saints' Church and was a member of the choir.

Mr. and Mrs. Wood have another son 12 years of age and two married daughters.

Ref. D.N.A.—Wills _2191._
_1939._

CERTIFICATE
OF THE INSPECTOR OF SEAMEN'S WILLS.

ADMIRALTY, the 31ˢᵗ day of _August_ 1950.

NOTE

This Certificate should be carefully kept and not destroyed or mislaid.

In pursuance of Act of Parliament 28th and 29th Vic., cap 111, and Order in Council 28th December, 1865, which provide that the Naval Assets of any deceased COMMISSIONED OFFICER, WARRANT OFFICER, PENSIONER, CIVILIAN, or OTHER PERSON mentioned therein, belonging to or having belonged to a Naval Establishment, when not exceeding One Hundred Pounds, may be paid without Letters of Administration or Probate of Will being taken out, if the claimant's right has been duly investigated and allowed by the Inspector of Seamen's Wills, whose Certificate sanctioning payment is to have the same force and effect as, and the payment on its authority be as valid and conclusive as if made under, Probate or Letters of Administration; I HEREBY CERTIFY THAT THE APPLICATION OF.....................

Mrs Eleanor Wood,

residing at _29 Kinny's Avenue,_

Langley Park, County Durham

claiming as _lawful mother and one of the persons entitled to share in the estate and to the legal representation undetermined_ the Effects of the late _Jack Wood,_

an Ordinary Seaman, Royal Navy, O.N.P/J.X. 157026.

.....................who died _intestate, a bachelor_.....................on the _14ᵗʰ October 1939,_

has been duly verified and attested as prescribed by the Order in Council, and the statements therein appearing to be true, that the said Claimant is entitled to receive what is due on account of the deceased in the Naval Department (it not exceeding ONE HUNDRED POUNDS), in order to administer the same according to Law.

for Inspector of Seamen's Wills.

Description of Effects for which this Certificate is granted.	Amount.			Mode and Date of Payment.
	£	s.	d.	
Naval Prize Money.	4	4	—	N.B. 51607 of 12.SEP. 1950

Chapter 9

Survivors of HMS *Royal Oak*

The following is taken from the account (published in *The Orcadian*, 18th October 2001) of an ordinary seaman (Able Seaman Stanley Ivan Cole) who, at the age of 18, survived the sinking of HMS *Royal Oak* in Scapa Flow on 14th October 1939.

During the day and evening of 13th October, the men were kept busy taking on and stowing stores. Able Seaman Stanley Cole and a close mess-mate, Bill, from the Newcastle-on-Tyne area, turned in at about 21.00 hours. The last sounds to be heard were the duty working parties going through the mess-decks closing down the heavy hatches and watertight doors.

The first explosion woke all on the mess-deck and they swung out of their hammocks to see what it was all about. The story was that it was either a carbon monoxide bottle exploding or something in the paint store – right forward. Some even said the anchor cable had snapped because of the rapidly deteriorating weather conditions. His mate Bill said, 'I don't like this, I'm going up top', and off he went; he never saw him again. Believing the situation to be not serious, many turned in again, but about 10 minutes later, he heard two very loud explosions, separated by only seconds, and the ship began to list and the lighting failed. Secondary lights working off batteries did not seem to be very effective and there began a crush of men making for the ladder to the next deck up. He had pulled on his overall suit over his underpants and attempted to grab his plimsolls but they slid down the sloping mess-deck, out of sight. There was a lot of milling and jostling at the foot of the ladder and he was aware of a lighter being struck and a voice of authority calling for no panic. By the feeble light, he could just make out a face and a Chief

Able Seaman Stanley Ivan Cole. Orkney Library Photographic Archives

Petty Officer's cap. His abandon-ship station was to report to the port-side whaler – one of the battleship's boats. He was one of the crew of five men on the oars, in charge of a coxswain, usually a leading seaman.

The boat deck was several decks up. Stanley, still not thinking the ship would sink, although it was listing considerably, struggled to get through to the ladders; was concerned about the consequences of not being at his place of duty. Finally, gaining his objective, still in darkness, he soon established that he was the only one there and wondered why he had heard no orders or instruction over the ship's tannoy. The whaler weighed about a ton and a half and, due to the list, was pressed hard against the davits. He had to support himself by clinging to the guard-rails. Having no knife, he could not even cut through ropes for hoisting, or lowering, and it occurred to him that even if he had been able to, the boat could have crashed down the ship's side and sustained damage. It might even have crashed down on to some of the swimmers already in the water.

He decided it was time to go, although he still did not think the ship would sink. He pulled himself through the lower gap of the guard-rail and launched himself in a half dive, half slithering movement down the ship's side. He got so far down before his right foot became jammed in the guttering of the 'blister' (the anti-torpedo bulge, which seemed not to have been effective on the starboard side). He stayed trapped, head down, for several seconds until he was able to free himself by pushing with his hands before slipping on down into the water. He could smell the oil fuel and could not avoid getting some in his mouth, nose and ears, but he kept his eyes closed until he surfaced. Coughing and spluttering he became aware that his right foot and leg seemed to be hanging in the water as he began to swim away from the ship's side, along with some others.

It was like trying to swim through liquid tar and he was convinced he wasn't going to make it. The water was bitterly cold and, from all around him in the darkness, he could hear cries for help from injured, burned, despairing bodies. Kicking out as best he could with his good leg, he was sure he could feel bodies of drowned ship-mates under his foot. His hand caught something – a small piece of wood about 2 feet long by 6 inches wide – and he hung on to it in the blind faith that it would keep him afloat! He would probably have killed anyone who tried to take it from him! Then, another stroke of luck – what he took to be a five-gallon oil drum came within range and he tried to hold his arm over it as it slipped and rolled in the oil.

Finally, after what seemed like ages, he made out three or four bobbing heads paddling slowly along with a length of timber that he supposed could have been one of the 'deals' they had adapted for seating for the church services. He let go of the drum, but not his small scrap of wood and joined up with the lads paddling the deal. They tried shouting and singing with hoarse throats without success, growing ever colder and more exhausted. One of their number slipped off the plank and they never saw him again.

His last view of the battleship *Royal Oak* was of her keel, silhouetted against the dark sky-line. She appeared to have turned right over. Then, just as he had all but given up the struggle, along came a ship's whaler, and he felt himself being hauled over the boat's side and dumped, with two or three other lads on top of him, in a cold, sodden, oily heap. On the drifter *Daisy II*, skipper John Gatt and his crew were valiantly dragging scores of bodies from the water, until *Daisy* herself was in danger of capsizing under the sheer weight of numbers. The *Daisy* transferred them to the sea-plane carrier *Pegasus* whose crew did whatever they could for them: washing them down with hot, clean water and turning out their lockers for every item of spare clothing and anything else they could get hold of.

Stanley was treated by the sick-bay staff, who dressed his foot in wads of cotton wool and wooden splints, gave him shots of pain-killer, then lifted him into someone's vacated hammock. They opened their canteen to give the survivors whatever there was to be had – cigarettes, chocolate, biscuits – anything. The following morning they were transferred to the armed liner *Voltaire*, then on to the hospital ship *Abba*. His foot and leg had sustained fractures and were encased in plaster of paris.

Another harrowing story was how the boy seamen's mess-deck became a mass of flame from the burning cordite. Many of the boys, aged around 15, had joined the *Royal Oak* about three weeks before, from a shore training establishment. An able seaman was said to have gone back to the boy's mess-deck to help some of them to escape, only to lose his own life. One has to pay tribute to *Daisy II* and Skipper Gatt and his men, without whom many more would have died in one of the worst tragedies in British naval history.

Survival of Surgeon-Lieutenant Dick Caldwell RN

This is the story of a very lucky naval officer who escaped the sinking of the battleship *Royal Oak* and later on during the war the sinking of the 35,000 ton *Prince of Wales* in the Far East.

It was 1939 when he was posted to the *Royal Oak*. As he travelled up to Scapa Flow he felt everywhere there was the shadow of war: a feeling of unease, Chamberlain's speech about 'Peace in our time' really had a hollow ring to it.

In September when war was declared, Admiral Blagrove called all his officers together in the wardroom and gave them all champagne. He gave them the toast, 'Damnation to Hitler'. On the night of 13th October he had been playing poker and had been listening to gramophone records with two fellow officers he was never to see again.

At half past twelve he picked his way carefully along the darkened quarterdeck to the hatchway leading to his cabin, undressed and climbed onto his bunk. As we now know the battleship was in harbour – if such a term could be used to describe the wide, bleak waters of Scapa Flow. No thought of impending disaster could have been in anyone's mind when at ten past one a muffled, ominous explosion shook the ship. With heart thumping he jumped down from his bunk, looked into the next cabin and saw his neighbour pulling on a pair of trousers.

Out in the cabin flat five or six officers were already discussing how and where the explosion could have occurred. Eight minutes passed, it was freezing cold, and one or two officers drifted back to their cabins. Just as he decided to do the same, a tremendous shuddering explosion occurred and the ship began to list to starboard. The tinkling of glass was heard as pictures fell from ledges and afterwards there seemed to be an awe-stricken silence – a silence that was suddenly shattered by a third explosion. All the lights went out, the list increased and it was obvious to everyone that all hope of saving the battleship had gone.

He got on to the deck in his pyjamas, monkey jacket and one bedroom slipper – he had dropped the other and remembered deciding not to retrieve it. A fourth torpedo struck them and the mighty bulk of the battleship shuddered again and settled further into the water. Those last three blows had occurred in the short space of three minutes and it was now every man for himself in a sinking ship with the cold, black sea all around them. He stood with others on the sloping deck in the darkness, wisps of smoke eddying round them. There were sudden splashes as men clambered over the guard rails and dived twenty or thirty feet into the water below.

His mind was curiously blank with regard to his personal safety. He had no plan, although he vividly recalls every thought and impression that passed through his brain, his new and rather expensive tennis racquet, a book that he had borrowed and promised to return, three pounds in the bottom of his drawer. A ship of this size must surely take a long time to sink. (Six minutes later it was out of sight.)

The ship suddenly increased her list more and more rapidly – they were now on the ship's side, and as she slid over, turning turtle, he lost his footing, fell, tried frantically to scramble up and dive clear and was thrown headlong into the sea. He seemed to go down and down and started fighting for breath. Then, as he came to the surface, the stem and propeller soared above him, then slipped slowly into the water and disappeared.

A torrent of water swept him head over heels. He went under again and came up in thick black oil. He gulped it and retched at the filthy taste of it in his throat. Oil, thick black oil, smarting in his eyes. He swam and floundered about, hoping to find some form of support in the darkness. None of them had lifebelts. He heard cries around him, saw many black heads bobbing, and he swam frantically again. He tried to wriggle out of his jacket, but found it heavy and slimy with oil. He repeatedly went under until quite suddenly he gave it up and thought, 'I'm going to drown'. He thought of all the people he wanted to see again and things he wanted to do – that was all he thought of – and then he saw a group of heads and threshed his way towards them.

Somebody swam quite strongly past him and he caught his leg and tried to hold it. The man kicked him clear. He then saw an upturned boat ahead of him. How far was it? Or how near? Fifteen yards can seem insurmountable. And then he touched the freeboard and held on. 'I've made it, by God, I've made it', and to think a few minutes before he might have been drowned.

He tried to wipe the oil out of his eyes with his free hand and then with his sleeve and realised how stupid that was.

There were about a dozen men hanging on round a boat which kept steady as long as they did, but every now and then someone would try to improve their position or make themselves more secure by clambering onto the upturned keel. Then slowly but inevitably their support would begin to roll over and back they would slip into the water, clawing frantically for a fingerhold on the smooth surface and shouting at each other until the movement ceased and they were supported once more. This happened many times and every time meant a mouthful of oil and a thumping heart.

Time dragged on with no sign of them being picked up. They strained their eyes in the darkness for some glimmer of light, but none came. At last they saw a masthead light which grew brighter and then the blacker darkness of a boat moving slowly towards them. They shouted again and again.

When she was within twenty yards of them, they left their upturned boat and struck out in her direction. She had ropes hanging down which they tried to climb up. He remembered falling back into the sea twice. His hands were numb but he thought, 'Mustn't lose now, come on, mustn't lose now'. But he had absolutely no recollection whatsoever of finally succeeding – he found himself sitting on a hot grating in the engine room, shivering uncontrollably from the cold which he had not previously noticed – most of the survivors had this experience.

He stood up and vomited oil and salt water all over somebody sitting at his feet. He did this three times and apologised each time to the man. He didn't appear to worry much anyway. *Daisy II*, the *Royal Oak's* drifter, took them to the *Pegasus*, where they were given hot drinks and helped into hot baths and splashed and scrubbed. The crew of the *Pegasus* were very grand to them and when the survivors began to talk and recognise people and shake hands, they tried not to notice friends that were missing.

Recollections of Commander Claude Sclater RN

A letter arrived at my home in Manchester, signed Nigel Sclater son of Commander Claude Sclater RN now deceased. This letter was his recollection of what his father, Claude, and mother, told him about the sinking of the *Royal Oak*. His story is retold in the interest of posterity.

Claude, a 29 year old Lieutenant serving on the *Royal Oak* was on watch on the bridge of the battleship on the night of 13th October 1939. On completing his watch he went below to his cabin, got into his pyjamas and went to bed. Almost immediately he heard an explosion and rushed back up to the bridge. He was told, 'Everything's all right, old boy, go back to bed.' On his way back to his cabin, at about 0115 (14th October) there was another explosion as the second salvo of torpedoes struck the ship. He said that the interval between the first and second explosions was about 15 minutes. Within a few moments the ship started listing and the order was given to abandon ship. Claude, still in his pyjamas, slid down the side of the ship into the cold black sea of Scapa Flow, scraping himself quite badly on the barnacles. Within a few minutes the ship had sunk. Claude was now in the cold, oil-covered sea, but he was a strong swimmer and after about 40 minutes he was picked up by a drifter (presumably *Daisy II*) and taken ashore, then on to Kirkwall where he was looked after by Ella Stephen, the proprietor of the St Ola Hotel on the harbour front of Kirkwall.

On 14th October Claude's wife Helen was staying with her mother-in-law at her home in Odiham, Hampshire. Both Helen and Claude's mother were in the sitting room when the 6 o'clock news on the wireless came on. The headline was the sinking of the *Royal Oak*. For some reason granny did not hear the news, but she froze when there were no reports of survivors and feared the worst. It was a couple of days later before she knew Claude was alive. Some time later, perhaps a week or two, the survivors were evacuated by train from Wick to Inverness, and whilst the train was somewhere near Wick it was attacked by German dive bombers. There were some casualties.

All this happened only a month or so after the start of the Second World War with little action seen by Britain's forces for a further six months.

After the war, in 1947, Claude was posted to HMS *Pomona*, the Naval Shore Base at Lyness on the Orkney island of Hoy, as resident Naval Officer in Command of the base. He was instrumental, whilst in this post, in having the *Royal Oak* declared an official war grave.

Obituary *The Times*

Commander Claude Sclater, DSO and Bar, FRGS, who died on 20th April 1986 at the age of 76, had a distinguished Naval career both as a surveyor and wartime destroyer Commander. Educated at Twyford School, he went to the Royal Naval College, Dartmouth. In the 1930s he assisted with surveys of unchartered waters off Borneo and Malaya for which he was elected a Fellow of the Royal Geographical Society in 1933.

At the outbreak of was he was serving on the battleship *Royal Oak* and survived her torpedoing in Scapa Flow, being rescued from the sea.

Then followed three and a half years in command of destroyers in the Atlantic and Artic theatres in which he saw much action. In June 1942 he was commanding the World War I vintage destroyer *Wild Swan* returning alone to Plymouth when she was attacked by German dive bombers. Firing her Pom Pom and Lewis guns she shot down six of her attackers, a feat unsurpassed in a single ship action.

However, she sustained such damage that she eventually sank and the survivors were rescued from the sea 15 hours later, 31 having perished from exposure.

Sclater was awarded the DSO for his bravery and skill during this action. In December 1942, in command of the destroyer *Obdurate,* he took part in the Battle of the Barents Sea in which the convoy JW-51B was attacked by a strong German force consisting of the pocket battleship *Lutzow*, the heavy cruiser *Hipper* and six destroyers.

The British escorts carried out a series of feint torpedo attacks coming under heavy fire from *Hipper, Obdurate* herself being hit.

However, these tactics succeeded in their objective of protecting the convoy. Hitler was so enraged at the failure to destroy JW-51B that he threatened to scrap his entire fleet and sacked his Commander in Chief Admiral Raeder.

Sclater was awarded a Bar to his DSO for his role in the battle.

On returning to Britain he was appointed Chief Staff Officer, Antwerp and after the invasion of Europe he was responsible for restoring and working the port. For this he was awarded the Belgian Order of Officer of the Crown.

He was mentioned in despatches while in command of a division of minesweepers operating in the St Georges Channel.

Subsequently, while serving as Resident Naval Officer Orkney, he was instrumental in having the sunken *Royal Oak* in which 833 of his shipmates had perished, declared an official war grave.

On retiring from the Royal Navy in 1955, he became Domas Bursar of Kings College Cambridge, of which he was also made a Fellow. One of his major tasks was the supervision of restoration of College buildings.

The author is informed that due to his many wartime experiences within the Royal Navy, he suffered from constant nightmares and sleep loss, until his death.

A Survivor's Story
Ammunition and Cordite Always a Potential Death Hazard

At either end of the propelling machinery amidships was dispersed the main punch of the battleship, the reason for her existence – eight fifteen-inch guns in four turrets, two just forward of the engines, two just aft of the boilers. The guns were protected by armour which in places was thirteen inches thick. The turrets revolved on barbettes, again thickly armoured which went down several decks to the armoured belt, so that the shells and cordite charges coming up through them from the shell rooms and magazines below the waterline would be shielded during the dangerous passsage to the guns.

Each shell room in each turret held 208 fifteen-inch shells; the magazine next to it contained the appropriate number of cordite propellant charges. From above they were protected by the armoured deck, capped by the barbettes and turrets. If a single enemy shell or bomb broke through a weak point to explode the cordite in a magazine, the shell room would explode within seconds, probably setting off the next shell room as well. The result would be a double bang, a cloud of smoke half a mile high and virtually no survivors.

This could happen accidentally if the temperature of the cordite was allowed to rise. A ship could blow up at anchor with no enemy near. To avoid a cordite explosion a system of safety vents was fitted which would allow the burning cordite to escape through the ship to the air before it built up enough pressure to explode. The result would be a trail of havoc, of cindered corpses and terribly burnt men screaming in agony, but the ship would still be afloat and fighting.

The second explosion occurred directly below the boys' mess deck from which there were hardly any survivors. The third was directly below the stokers' mess; the last, after an interval, was aft again under the marines' mess deck.

The third explosion had caused the lights to fail and set an after magazine on fire. The burning cordite did not explode, it simply swept through the vents, seeking the quickest way to open air on the port side. By the 'heads' (toilets) an orange pillar of glittering flame soared up the hatch. It was cordite. This flame swept round and round inside the heads burning everyone there. The cordite flame was bright orange outside and an intense blue inside.

The flame roared about inside the ship aft between the 'heads' and the marines' mess deck . Part of it escaped to the open air through the blackout curtains leading from the port battery on the quarterdeck and vanished.

Anyone caught in the path of flaming cordite is incinerated within minutes. It moves too quickly to outrun it.

Chapter 10

SCAPA FLOW

AND THE CHURCHILL BARRIERS

At the heart of the Orkney Islands off Scotland's north coast lies the great open stretch of sea known as Scapa Flow. This vast basin, ten miles across at its widest point, forms a natural harbour between the North Sea to the east and the Atlantic Ocean to the west. The broken concrete that can still be seen in these islands bears witness to Scapa Flow's importance as the main naval base for the British Home Fleet in two world wars.

To the East of Scapa Flow, there were until World War II, four channels leading into the naval anchorage. These were blocked with sunken ships and it was considered that attack from that direction by sea was impossible. However, after the sinking of the battleship HMS *Royal Oak*, the Navy, having learned a hard lesson, left its Orkney anchorage until the entrances could be securely sealed. The method chosen was to lay massive barriers of stone and concrete on the seabed from island to island. The contractors were Balfour Beatty.

This enormous task took several years, the total length of the four sections of the barriers being about one and a half miles. In some places the depth of the water was as much as fifty-nine feet. As a foundation, more than a quarter of a million tons of stone and rock were laid on the seabed, and on top of this were built the causeways. They were constructed from 66,000 huge blocks of concrete, some weighing five tons and some ten tons. These blocks were placed in varying positions, all along either side of the barriers, their angles and crevices preventing the tide from sweeping over the carriage-way which runs along the top.

Building the Barriers at Scapa Flow

The Causeway at Scapa Flow

For over 60 years, HMS *Royal Oak* has lain undisturbed, a grave for the 833 men who died when the battleship was torpedoed by a U-boat.

The fight to preserve the dignity of the wreck in Scapa Flow has grown fiercer in recent years as the thousands of tonnes of oil seeping from the corroding hull threaten environmental disaster and death to Scapa Flow's large seal population and several species of rare birds. The natural action of the tide and winds is pushing the oil to the surface. Divers return to the wreck of the *Royal Oak* on a regular basis to check on oil still leaking from the battleship. To date, they believe there may be 1500 tonnes of fuel remaining trapped in the upturned ship, less than half the amount that was thought to have been in the ship's tanks when she sank.

Most recent efforts by divers working for the Ministry of Defence have involved 'hot tapping' the fuel tanks to drain the oil, but the process is slow. In the past three years, the 'tapping' has drawn 670 tonnes of oil from the ship. It is thought fuel seeps from inner tanks to the outer ones, from where it can be 'drawn off' without damaging the hull or harming its status as a National War Grave.

Royal Navy divers visit the wreck annually to carry out a survey and replace the white ensign, hoisting it under water. A moving memorial service and wreath-laying ceremony is also conducted near the site every year on the Saturday falling closest to the anniversary of her sinking. The remaining survivors and their families gather together at the Naval War Memorial on Southsea Common at her home base of Portsmouth to hold a service in memory of those who went down with this mighty battleship. The survivors, relatives and Orcadians all remember and respect. So must we all.

Chapter 11

'SPIES' AT SCAPA FLOW

Hereunder 'verbatim' is a letter from a former serving officer in the Royal Navy, now retired and residing in Cornwall.

> In about 1938, two Swedish yachtsmen in a converted fishing boat *Thalatta* took soundings and current speeds in entrance channels to Scapa Flow. I am over 90, so my memory is a bit rusty, but a photograph of them doing so was published in a Yachtsman's Annual (? *Yachting Monthly*) in 1937 or 1938.

> I did not see them personally as I was in another ship doing annual training, but a friend of mine told me about their activities. Some time later we asked a senior R.N. Officer, but he said it didn't matter, as many foreign yachts regularly appeared in these waters.

> During the war I served in two warships that swung around buoys in Scapa Flow (HMS *Bonaventure* and HMS *Prince of Wales*). My impression was that both captains were more concerned about keeping to a rigid obedience of rules than looking out for a naughty U-Boat sneaking in the back door.

> Unfortunately anyone likely to add to my story has passed on, but possibly my information might lead to your theory about spies. When HMS *Royal Oak* was lost, an old friend

A photograph of the Swedish-registered yacht, Thalatta

of mine Sub Lieutenant Peter James RNVR (Bristol
Division) went with her. In conclusion I hope my letter is
of interest.

In the event that there may be an element of truth about these
matters I decided to carry out some research to separate possible
truth from fiction.

From Gothenburg to Dublin and back
By Harald Hammersten
Translated by Ture Rinman

In the *Yachtsman's Annual and Who's Who* for the years 1938-39 is
an account of the above journey made by the Swedish registered
yacht *Thalatta* together with photographs taken by the Captain and
author Harald Hammersten.

The yacht was powered by a 25 horse power diesel engine.

During their journey to Dublin and back they encountered heavy
seas in the unpredictable notorious Pentland Firth and took
soundings and current speeds , and after navigating the various
channels, many of which had sunken block ships, entered the
relatively calm waters of Scapa Flow. My considered opinion is
that of a journey taken some months before the outbreak of World
War II with no sinister intent, but only to seek temporary refuge in
Scapa Flow prior to continuing their journey. It is certain that had
they attempted to make the journey in the early weeks leading up
to the war in 1939, the yacht and its crew would have been
challenged and made to account for their proximity to Scapa Flow,
probably prior to entering the Royal Navy anchorage from the
Pentland Firth direction.

Hitler Youth

I have in my possession a letter sent to me during April 2006 from
someone in Scotland who had joined the RAF VR just before World
War II. He says that his first posting was to RAF 100 Wing Sullom
Voe Shetland.

To reach his final destination took him five days. He travelled from Pittenweem to Perth by bus, and then boarded a train, which took him to Inverness, and from Inverness to Thurso. From Thurso the Royal Navy transported him by road to Scrabster where he boarded the St Ola ferry sailing across the Pentland Firth to enter Scapa Flow after a trawler opened up the boom to let them in. They then proceeded into Kirkwall. From Kirkwall he boarded the ferry St Clair and proceeded to Berwick, Shetland, where RAF transport was waiting to take him to Sullom Voe.

We now proceed to his story of the six canoes.

In the summer of 1938, with World War II imminent, he apparently came across a crowd of locals, between the harbour and the house on the rocks. He does not say which harbour, but that these locals were waving to six boys in canoes shouting, '*Auf Wiedersehen*'. Asking what it was all about, he was told that six German boys from 'Hitler Youth' were going around the coast in canoes.

As they paddled away, he muttered that he did not trust these 'German buggers'. They had all been told later on whilst at Sullom Voe, that the *Royal Oak* had been sunk with the loss of 833 lives, and that a German submarine had slipped into Scapa Flow when the boom had been opened to allow a ship in, but in fact, he says that the submarine had sailed 'over the breakwater' at a special place, and goes on to ask, 'How did the Germans know?' Did the six canoes find this special place? Someone must have been supervising these boys, and why were members of the 'Hitler Youth' allowed in Scotland when we were so close to war. Yet another mystery surrounding the *Royal Oak*.

The Spy Who Never Was

When visiting Orkney in September 2003, I was absolutely astounded to learn, from an Orcadian who wished to remain anonymous, a story concerning espionage in relation to the sinking of the battleship HMS *Royal Oak*.

The Admiralty, deeply embarrassed and humiliated by the sinking of the *Royal Oak* in its own anchorage in Scapa Flow, assumed that *U-47* had been guided to its target by a spy in Orkney.

Vernon Kell, director of MI5, c.1919.
Sources: H. Keith Melton and Nigel West

MI5, the British counter-intelligence service, was promptly blamed by the Admiralty for failing to flush out the Nazi spy. MI5 agents descended en masse on Orkney in an attempt to find the elusive spy who had made this German exploit possible. The search failed.

I am indebted to Curt Reiss, an American journalist and espionage scholar for the following astounding report.

In the Spring of 1942, the *Saturday Evening Post* published an article identifying the Scapa Flow spy as a former officer of the German Imperial Navy, Kapitän Alfred Wehring. According to the *Post* account, Wehring had been recruited in 1928 by German intelligence to be its man at Scapa Flow, which, it was believed, would be a crucial location in any coming war against the British. Wehring adopted the fictitious name of Albert Oertal, posed as a Swiss watchmaker and opened a small shop in the town of Kirkwall in the Orkneys.

Twelve years later, Wehring emerged from deep undercover and signalled to Kapitän Karl Dönitz of the U-boat Command detailed intelligence about Scapa Flow's defences, its unpredictable currents and its navigation obstacles.

Wehring is reported to have boarded *U-47* at the mouth of Scapa Flow, acted as a Pilot-Navigator, then returned to Germany in triumph after twelve years of deep undercover intelligence work in Scotland and Orkney.

After the war, Major General Vernon G. W. Kell, then head of MI5, wrote that: 'The Germans had been supplied with up to date information by a spy.' In England, with peace coming nearly six years after the *Royal Oak* had been sunk, controversy continued to swirl around the event. The Admiralty it seems still clings to the strong contention that Wehring (Oertal) had been the culprit.

British journalists probing into the affair, descended on Orkney and failed to locate anyone who had ever known of, much less seen Alfred Wehring, who for twelve years was said to have been masquerading in Kirkwall as Albert Oertal, a Swiss watchmaker. Kapitän-leutnant Günther Prien is probably the one man who could have provided precise information.

So the question remains. Had there really been a Nazi undercover spy long embedded in the fabric of life in Orkney? A German who performed one of history's boldest espionage feats? Or was it only The Spy who Never Was?

Despite further extensive research at the highest level of security, no evidence exists today to suggest that Prien received information or assistance from a spy working for German intelligence, based in Scotland to enable him to successfully carry out his mission to penetrate the defences at Scapa Flow and sink the battleship *Royal Oak*. It had always been considered a suicidal attempt and *U-47* was carrying sufficient quantities of explosives with strict orders to blow itself up if there was any risk of the boat being captured by the British.

It was a stupendous maritime feat and a colossal propaganda victory for the Third Reich.

In my research, I have recently been in discussion with the Security Service MI5 and the Home Office to establish if Prien did receive assistance from a German spy based in Scotland, prior to his sinking in 1939.

The Intelligence Service believe that there is no basis for the SS General Walther Schellenberg claim that a German spy provided the *Abwehr* with intelligence enabling the German navy to sink the *Royal Oak*. Indeed, they are as certain as may be that he made the story up. Moreover, there is no reference to a Scapa Flow spy in their historical archive, no record of those named in the various versions of the story they have seen in either MI5 records or in Home Office records.

Professor Andrew, the MI5 historian believes in addition to the above, that had there been a spy of the sort alleged, historical details would have emerged by now.

Post-war researches in *Abwehr* and German naval records also drew a blank so far as this spy story is concerned.

Surprisingly no mention or information was forthcoming in relation to Major General Vernon G.W. Kell's statement. I have been invited by Professor Andrew to consult Dr Thomas Boghardt, historian at the International Spy Museum in Washington DC who has researched German espionage archives and is a world authority on 'Spies of the Kaiser' for confirmation of the facts as presented to me by the Security Service MI5.

The Department of the Chief of Naval Information, Whitehall

had on 20th October 1958, stated:

> The story of the 'Watchmaker Spy of Kirkwall' is a fairy tale.

The Germans also strongly deny the story, which makes it unanimous. There was, however, a Watchmaker and Jeweller in Orkney, Mr W Hourston of 34, Albert Street, Kirkwall, who gave a signed statement dated 18th February 1959.

> As a Jeweller and Watchmaker who has been in business in Kirkwall all my life, and a citizen whose knowledge of Kirkwall throughout the years has been complete, I certify with the utmost assurance that never at any period has there been a Watchmaker in Kirkwall known as Albert Oertel, or any person connected in any way with the Trade who could possibly be identified with the mystical 'Watchmaker Spy of Kirkwall'. I am convinced beyond possibility of doubt that such a person has never existed and is only a journalist's fabrication.

No Spy on Orkney?

If there was no spy on Orkney, what was the source of the information on the basis of which Dönitz decided upon the attack and prepared his operations plan? It was on 6th September 1939, when the war with Britain was only three days old, that Dönitz began to collect the data he needed for the planning of the operation. Later in September, Lieutenant Commander Wellner returned in *U-16* from a war cruise to the Orkney Islands. Since this was still Hitler's deceptive era of goodwill, when he hoped to restore peace with Britain, he had banned all offensive U-Boat operations against the British. Wellner spent his time on the cruise in reconnoitring the waters around the Orkney Islands and observing enemy activities in them. He ventured quite close to Hoxa and Switha Sounds in the south, which he found more or less blocked, and to Holm Sound where he found conditions somewhat different. He discovered the hulks of three merchant ships in Kirk Sound, but also spotted a narrow channel about 50 feet wide running as far as

Land Holm, which appeared to be comparatively open, except for a few stray sunken ships.

Upon his return to his base in Wilhelmshaven, Commander Wellner gave Dönitz 'a detailed report' not only of these findings, but also 'on the patrols', the lighting and the prevalent currents in the area.

As we know from MI5 intelligence, 'Captain Wehring' never existed as a supposed spy at Scapa Flow, but there was a real-life spy working for Commander Menzel of the naval intelligence division at *Abwehr* headquarters.

Menzel arranged a trip to the Orkney Islands for one of his most astute men, a merchant navy captain, who doubled as an *Abwehr* spy. This spy was Captain Horst Kahle, skipper of the Neptune Freighter *Theseus*. From a trip to Kirkwall in late August, just before the commencement of war, Kahle returned with a fairly complete account, describing the shore on both sides of Land Holm as 'practically uninhabited'. He also reported that no anti-aircraft batteries had been placed anywhere along the southern coast as far as the western shore of the mainland where, however, he had spotted three sets of heavy AA guns.

The neglected state of Scapa's defences was constantly being talked about in Kirkwall. Such things as the boom and anti-torpedo defences, guard and mine loops, indicator loops and anti-boat nets were either in bad repair or non-existent in the Eastern approaches.

This was basically the sum total of the intelligence which Dönitz had available to him when he concluded that 'here (through Kirk Sound) it would be possible to penetrate – by night, on the surface at slack water'. He then prepared his operation plan for the attack, and handed it to Prien to execute it.

One has to wonder why the British authorities accepted the story of a spy who we now almost certainly know did not exist in Scotland. It is possible that because Admiralty investigators were told that some unidentified person in a car with headlights blazing had driven along the southern mainland road in an East-West direction when *U-47* was approaching Scapa Flow, giving some substance to the theory that Prien had a guide on the shore.

Whatever the reason behind such apparent gullibility, it was to have an influence on the personal fortunes of Major General Vernon Kell, the head of MI5. The mysterious events surrounding the sinking of the *Royal Oak* was seized upon as one of the excuses to get rid of Kell and finally he was summoned to 10 Downing Street and asked to resign. He died 'unknown to the public and forgotten by authority'.

I have found no Alfred Wehring, Captain or otherwise, in any of the registers of either the German Imperial Navy, the post-war navy or the *Abwehr*.

I can find no evidence relating to Albert Oertel in the documents of the naval intelligence divisions of either World Wars or of the *Abwehr*.

There is no evidence that either the *Abwehr* or any other German intelligence agency ever had an operative stationed in Kirkwall or the Orkney Islands.

However, it is alleged the first Nazi spy of World War II was caught and arrested at Duncansby Head noting the movements of British warships in and out of Scapa Flow. I have in my possession a letter from a lady residing in Wick who says that her late husband and his sister remember 'the German spy' who lodged with their parents, William and Elizabeth Rosie at Sunsay, Wick. The man was apparently a piano tuner, spoke with an English accent and said that he came from London. He spent a lot of his time at Duncansby Head, carrying with him at all times the tools of his trade together with a smaller case. He eventually left and they were later informed that he had been arrested on his way to the West coast.

Although I have been given free access to official documents in relation to British intelligence in World War II, including the names of various *Abwehr* agents, I have been unable to unearth any information which directly connects with this particular case.

There were many spies operating throughout the British Isles prior to and during the War. Many aliens were resident within the country. Some were deported, others were confined to special prisons for the duration of the War. Arrests of spies were made in

Scotland – three from a seaplane that landed in the Moray Firth, others in Glasgow and Edinburgh. The first German spies to arrive in Britain did so at Dungeness and Dymchurch in Kent on 3rd September 1940, having been brought across the Channel by a fishing boat. They were quickly caught.

Spies were operating within most major towns and cities, especially areas of stategic importance. Most were quickly apprehended before they had time to provide the *Abwehr* with vital information. Some were acquitted due to lack of evidence, others were 'turned over' to work for MI5. The majority were tried under the Treachery Act and executed.

On the deck of Royal Oak – ship's mascot
Permission: The Trustees of the Imperial War Museum, London Q 017983

104 LOOKING FORWARD

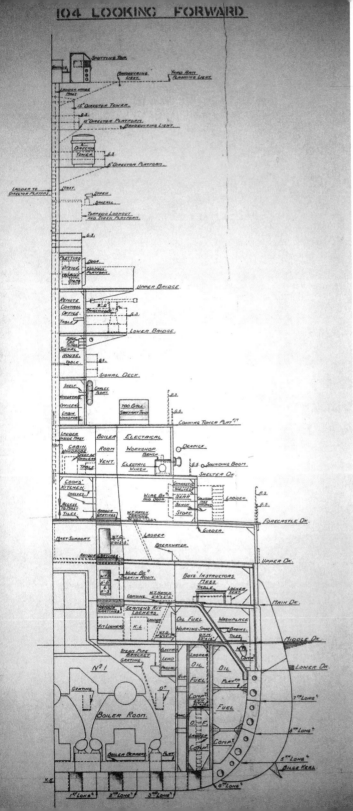

Architectural
drawing of
HMS Royal Oak

Permission:
National
Maritime
Museum

Chapter 12

WORLD WAR II BRITISH BATTLESHIPS

Projections for new battleships provided a distinctly bleak outlook in the decade after World War I. For although on paper they had an enormous superiority in numbers, the older dreadnoughts were weakly armed and protected in comparison with the new Japanese and American battleships.

The British Hood design was a follow-on from the Queen Elizabeth design, a fast battleship rather than a battle-cruiser with 12-inch armour and a speed of 31 knots. Although she incorporated many new features such as inclined armour, her design was too far advanced for all the lessons of Jutland to be incorporated and, as a result, her deck protection was not adequate against long-range shell-fire. The Director of Naval Construction regarded the design as inadequate in the light of wartime experience. The Admiralty,

Admiralty Projections for New Battleships in 1920

Quantity	Type	Tonnage	Number x Size of Guns	Top Speed
4	Hood Class	41,200 tons	8 x 15 inch	31 knots
2	Repulse	27,000 tons	6 x 15 inch	31 knots
5	Revenge	29,150 tons	8 x 15 inch	22 knots
5	Queen Elizabeth	27,500 tons	8 x 15 inch	24 knots
4	Iron Duke	25,000 tons	10 x 13.5 inch	21 knots
3	King George V	23,000 tons	10 x 13.5 inch	21 knots
4	Orion	22,000 tons	10 x 13.5 inch	21 knots
1	Tiger	28,500 tons	8 x 13.5 inch	30 knots

therefore, gave up all thought of completing work on the three modified sisters of the *Hood*.

The Admiralty had hoped to order three new 43,500 ton battleships armed with nine 18-inch guns and a 48,000 ton battle-cruiser with nine 16-inch guns in the 1921-1922 financial year and the same number of ships the following year. However, the existing battle-cruisers were so weakly protected that the Board revised the programme to four battle-cruisers in the 1921-1922 programme and four battleships to follow in 1922-1923.

British Battleship Losses 1939-1945

HMS *Royal Oak*	14th October 1939	Torpedoed, Scapa Flow by *U-47*
HMS *Hood*	24th May 1941	Destroyed in *Bismarck* action
HMS *Barham*	25th November 1941	Torpedoed, Med. Sea by *U-331*
HMS *Prince of Wales*	10th December 1941	Air attack, Malaya
HMS *Repulse*	10th December 1941	Air attack, Malaya

As the most expensive and advanced ships of their time, battle-ships could only be built by the leading nations and the threat of a battleship's guns was a potent political instrument.

HMS *Warspite*, Flagship of the Mediterranean Fleet, was probably the most famous British battleship of World War II.

The British followed the strategy that had proved so successful in World War I, moving the home fleet to Scapa Flow to block the exits to the Atlantic. However, this time the great fleet base did not prove immune to attack.

The *Bismarck*

On 20th May 1941, the *Bismarck*, whose size, power and awe-inspiring name made her the most feared of all German battleships, left the Baltic for the Atlantic to prey on British convoys. On 24th May, she was intercepted by the battleship HMS *Prince of Wales* and the battlecruiser HMS *Hood*. The German battleship concentrated its fire on the *Hood*, which blew up after a salvo of shells detonated her ammunition magazines. Only three of the *Hood's* 1,418 man crew survived. The *Prince of Wales* scored several hits

HMS Acasta

HMS Despatch

but was damaged. Several other Royal Naval ships were deployed to shadow and to sink the *Bismarck*, including *King George V* and *Rodney* who were sailing from the north.

The Commander-in-Chief of the home fleet in the *King George V* signalled to all ships involved in the engagement saying, 'Intend to engage the enemy at dawn from the westward with the *Rodney*'.

The sun rose at 07:15, but the light and visibility were very poor due to constant rain squalls and low clouds and it was not until 08:30 that the Commander decided conditions were good enough.

The Bismarck

Bismarck survivors being rescued by a Royal Navy ship

The *King George V* opened fire, then the *Rodney*, with answering fire from the *Bismarck*. Having been hit by torpedo from the destroyer *Cossack*, *Bismarck's* forecastle was on fire and her speed reduced to seven or eight knots. The *Dorsetshire* was ordered to sink her with torpedoes. Thus ended a very gallant *Bismarck* and a brave ship's company. They had fought until there was not a gun in action and their ship nothing but a battered hulk.

The battleships *King George V*, the *Prince of Wales*, the battle-cruisers HMS *Hood*, and HMS *Sheffield*, aircraft carriers *Ark Royal* and *Renown* and several destroyers including the *Cossack*, *Maori* and *Zulu*, all played a part in this, one of the biggest sea battles of World War II, leading to the German battleship's eventual destruction. Only 116 of the Bismarck's crew of 2,200 survived the battle.

HMS Hood, a battlecruiser built in 1918, at anchor in Scapa Flow in 1940

The beautiful but ill-fated Hood, intended to be a 31-knot version of the Queen Elizabeth, she remained the largest capital ship in the world until her loss

HMS Nelson firing her starboard 6-inch secondary guns in 1940

HMS Renown seen in 1940 after complete reconstruction. She carried an external degaussing cable for protection against magnetic mines

HMS Warspite, the flagship of the Mediterranean Fleet and the most famous battleship of World War II, with a seven-destroyer escort, it sank eight German destroyers in the second Battle of Narvik, April 13th, 1940

HMS Barham in Gibraltar in September 1940. She had received only a superficial modernisation and new machinery between the wars. On November 25th, 1941 the U-331 hit the Barham amidships with three torpedoes from such close range that the submarine was blown to the surface. The Barham exploded with a loss of 862 lives

The End of Force Z

On 10th December 1941, the Force Z South China Sea battleship, *Prince of Wales*, and the battlecruiser *Repulse*, escorted by the destroyers *Express, Electra* and *Vampire*, were spotted by the Japanese submarine *I-65*, while racing to meet the Japanese invasion fleet at Kuantan, Malaya. Aircraft scouts from the cruisers *Kinu* and *Kumano* reported that the fleet had no air cover. Ninety-five aircraft from the 22nd air flotilla took off from Saigon.

They found first the destroyer *Tenedos* but she escaped their bombs and proceeded. In the main attack on Force Z, two aerial torpedoes crippled the screws and rudder of the *Prince of Wales*; the *Repulse*, although damaged, managed to avoid seventeen torpedoes before being struck by eight more. Direct hits with three torpedoes and nine bombs were made on the *Prince of Wales*. Both ships were doomed. The destroyers rescued 1,924 men and took them to Singapore.

The end of Force Z marked the end of the era of the battleship. No new battleships have since been ordered by any navy.

12-29th March 1941

The British Mediterranean fleet led by the battleships *Barham,*

Valiant and *Warspite* fought the 'Battle of Matapan' at night and sank three Italian cruisers and three destroyers.

19th December 1941
As if to underline the vulnerability of the battleship, two Italian 'human torpedoes' breached the harbour defences at Alexandria and badly damaged the British battleships *Queen Elizabeth* and *Valiant* with limpet mines.

26th December 1943
The sinking of the *Scharnhorst* while it was trying to get through to attack the Arctic convoy JW-55B was the last battle of World War II in which a British battleship was involved. After the *Scharnhorst* had been hit by torpedoes from three British destroyers, the battleship *Duke of York* fired her guns from close range and sank the German ship.

HMS Duke of York in her prime, serving in the Home Fleet in 1949

HMS Duke of York comes alongside the quay at the end of her last voyage to the breakers in 1958

HMS Vanguard firing a salvo from her 15-inch guns. Her flared forecastle made her a magnificent sea-boat. The last and best of the long line of British battleships, she carried the most comprehensive outfit of AA guns: no fewer than 72 Bofors guns, most of which were in six-barrelled radar-controlled mountings

One of the four King George V class battleships, HMS Anson, leaving the Gare Loch on the Clyde in 1958, bound for the scrapyard. Two years later, she would be followed by the Vanguard

HMS Anson, 1945

HMS Nelson, 1942

HMS Barham, 1934

HMS Prince of Wales, 1941

HMS Repulse

HMS Queen Elizabeth, 1943

HMS Vanguard

HMS Warspite

EPITAPH

Like a sleeping giant the Royal Oak lay,
When U-forty seven struck.
Three 'eels' were fired, two lost their way,
But with one there was some luck.

Reload the tubes, Prien's order came,
Prepare another fan of three.
Down came the chain hoist from above
As the sub ploughed through the sea.

Attack – the order turned the bows
Towards the sleeping ship.
Endrass bent over the optic aim,
Felt the submarine turn and dip.

Doors reopened, the eels jumped out.
Three torpedoes from the bow
Towards the Royal Oak's starboard side
That was closing faster now.

The great ship shuddered, lifted up,
Then she gently settled back.
Lights flickered out, fans stopped running,
All power she did lack.

Across the decks the water flowed,
And a sheet of orange flame
Exploded beneath the starboard deck,
Impossible to restrain.

Thick black smoke rose o'er the port,
Bulkheads shuddered and cracked
Decks caved in and swirling flames
Rose from the cruel impact.

Through doors and hatches men were blown,
From hot ladders they were flung,
In hammocks brutally devoured by fire,
Their flesh from the cabin walls it clung.

Her death throes over, the Royal Oak
Plunged beneath the waves.
A tomb for several hundred men,
For few that day were saved.

Silently the submarine slipped
Out to the ocean deep,
Leaving Scapa Flow and the Royal Oak
To the nightmares of their sleep.

Reproduced with kind permission
Colin F. Forbes, 2002

ACKNOWLEDGEMENTS

I am indebted to many people without whom this book would have been impossible to write. To preserve their privacy, a very small number of them have asked that their contribution remain anonymous. I am glad to be able to make a public debt of gratitude to the following:

Alan S Wakefield, Curator Photographic Archive, Imperial War
    Museum, London;
Charlie Millar, BEM, Royal British Legion, Kirkwall;
Commander C.W. Crighton, OBE;
Commonwealth War Graves Commission;
Craig Wilson, STV North;
David Mackie, Photographic Archivist, Orkney Museum,
    Kirkwall;
Elizabeth Dickson, daughter of Johnnie Duthie, Fraserburgh;
Evening Herald, Plymouth;
Hazel Deans, STV North;
Jeremy Michell, Curator Historic Photographs and Ships Plans,
    National Maritime Museum, Greenwich, London;
Johnnie Duthie, Fraserburgh, crew member of the drifter, *Daisy
    II*, and author of *Lest We Forget*, published by P. Scrogie Ltd,
    Peterhead;
Ken Amer, freelance photographer and cameraman, Orkney;
Lewis Munro, Custodian, Scapa Flow Visitor Centre and Royal
    Navy Museum, Lyness;
Naval Historical Branch, MOD, London;
Plymouth Naval Base, Devonport;
Rob Jaskowski, Granada Television, Manchester;

Royal Navy's Environmental Unit, Bath;
The Orcadian, Kirkwall, Orkney;
Tom Muir, Curator, Orkney Museum, Kirkwall;
Yolande M Turner, Manchester.

Also special thanks to Charlie Kemp, Kirkwall, for our unforgettable evening flight over Scapa Flow, the wreck of the Royal Oak and the Churchill Barriers.

BIBLIOGRAPHY

Manuscript and archival sources
Records of the Admiralty
Records of the Home Office
Records of the Ministry of Defence
Records of the MI5 Security Intelligence Service
Memoirs of Grand Admiral Dönitz
U-Boat archive – Cuxhaven Germany
House of Lords Record Office
His Majesty's Ship *Royal Oak* Inquiry Oral Answers House of
    Commons, 17 October 1939 – 25 October 1939.
List of Neville Chamberlain's Cabinet, September 1939

Atlantic U-boat, Type VII

1 Superstructure
2 Pressure hull
3 Main deck
4 Forward hatch
5 Officers' quarters
6 Tower compartment
7 Bridge
8 Sky periscope
9 Direction finder
10 Attack periscope
11 Anti-aircraft guns (2cm)
12 Anti-aircraft guns (3.7cm)
13 Rudder
14 Rear hydroplanes and twin screws
15 Motor room and aft torpedo tube
16 Diesel room
17 Galley and washroom
18 Petty officers' quarters
   and Battery I below deck

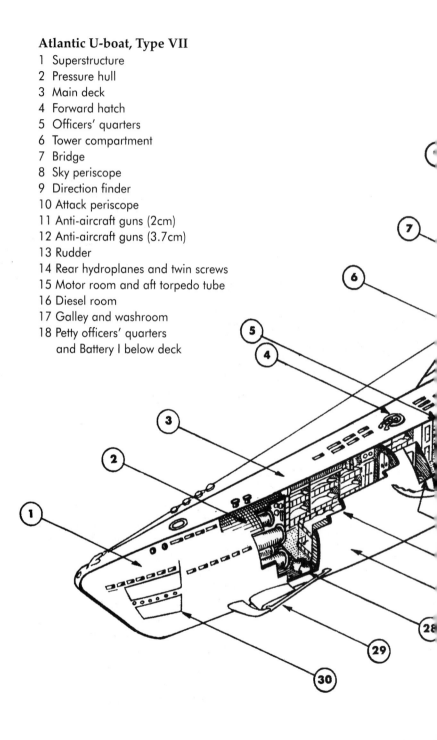

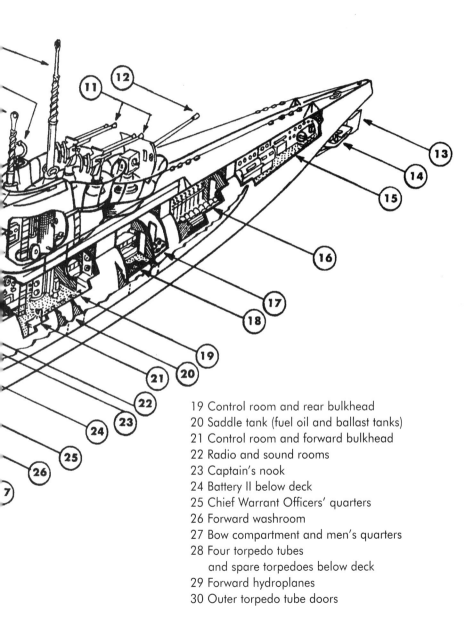

19 Control room and rear bulkhead
20 Saddle tank (fuel oil and ballast tanks)
21 Control room and forward bulkhead
22 Radio and sound rooms
23 Captain's nook
24 Battery II below deck
25 Chief Warrant Officers' quarters
26 Forward washroom
27 Bow compartment and men's quarters
28 Four torpedo tubes
   and spare torpedoes below deck
29 Forward hydroplanes
30 Outer torpedo tube doors

About the author

Born in Plymouth the eldest son of a senior civil servant to the Admiralty, David Turner left the city with his brother having suffered bombing by the German Luftwaffe during the early days of World War II.

Educated at Wellingborough, Glossop and Urmston Grammar Schools and RAF Cranwell, he continued his associaton with aviation until leaving British European Airways in 1954.

Qualified in engineering and marketing, he has held several senior posts in industry, in cluding the British Steel Corporation. His leisure activitues are antiquarian horology, history, art, golf and snooker.

He has lived in the north-west of England for many years and has contributed to radio and television news programmes in England and Scotland.

Last Dawn is the outcome of meticulous research into the events surrouding the death of his uncle during the tragic sinking of HMS *Royal Oak* in 1939.